# THE GOLDEN AGE OF
# BASEBALL

## 1941-1963

# THE GOLDEN AGE OF
# BASEBALL
## 1941-1963

### BILL GUTMAN

GALLERY BOOKS
An imprint of W.H. Smith Publishers Inc.
112 Madison Avenue
New York, New York 10016

Published by Gallery Books
A Division of W H Smith Publishers Inc.
112 Madison Avenue
New York, New York 10016

Produced by
Brompton Books Corp.
15 Sherwood Place
Greenwich, CT 06830

ISBN 0-8317-3911-8

Printed in Hong Kong

10 9 8 7 6 5 4 3 2 1

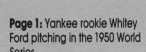

**Page 1:** Yankee rookie Whitey
Ford pitching in the 1950 World
Series.

**Page 2-3:** Monte Irvin of the
Giants stealing home.

**Page 4-5:** Garagiola, Sisler,
Kurowski, Slaughter and Musial
of 1946 Cards.

# INTRODUCTION

It was a Golden Age in many ways. It began at a time when the game of baseball was entering the new decade of the 1940s with bright optimism. The great names of baseball's early period were all retired: Cobb, Ruth, Johnson, Wagner, Young, Mathewson, Speaker, Alexander, Hornsby, Lajoie, Traynor, Collins, Terry, Frisch and others. They were all players from the early days of the century, fixtures through the growth years of the 1920s and into the 1930s. In addition, a number of other great players were winding down their careers at the outset of the new decade. Future Hall of Famers such as Jimmie Foxx, Charlie Gehringer, Lefty Grove, Paul Waner, Carl Hubbell, Dizzy Dean and Al Simmons were all getting ready to call it quits.

The Lou Gehrig tragedy would end with the death of the Yankees' Iron Horse in June 1941. But the cyclical nature that has always kept the game fresh and exciting was continuing to weave its magic. By the time the new decade had arrived, the game of baseball had yet another generation of great young players on the scene, men who looked more than ready to challenge some of the records set by earlier players.

Attendance was up as well as the 1940s began. The American League set a new mark when 5,433,791 fans pushed through the turnstiles in the first year of the new decade, and nearly 4,400,000 attended National League games. Young superstars such as Joe DiMaggio, Ted Williams and Bob Feller were already making an impact on the sport and would continue to do so in years to come. But the game of baseball, as well as everything else, would soon find there was no way to go about business as usual. World War II would see to that.

**Below:** Yankee Joe DiMaggio rounds first after hitting in his 42nd straight game, en route to 56.

**Below right:** Ted Williams of the Rex Sox, one of the greatest hitters of all-time.

The War Years of 1942-1945 altered the game in a way that had never been seen before. Bob Feller, who had won 25 games for the Cleveland Indians in 1941, was the first of the big-name players to enlist in the service, signing up shortly after the Japanese attack on Pearl Harbor. He was followed by a mass exodus that seriously depleted the ranks of all the teams and diluted the quality of play.

But the game continued throughout the war and, as usual, endured. And when the War ended baseball boomed. People were looking for a release from the anxieties and tragedies that were the hallmarks of war, and baseball provided the perfect tonic. Many of the great players returned to resume their careers, while still others joined the ranks of the big league's best.

Then, just two years after the war, when the game had returned to so-called normalcy, there was an event that would change the entire face of baseball for years to come. In fact, it was an event of such proportions that it can be said finally to have made baseball a true "national" pastime.

It happened in 1947 when Branch Rickey, the man who ran the Brooklyn Dodgers, brought to the team a rookie second baseman named Jackie Robinson. Before 1947 there had never been a black man in the big leagues.

It was a bold move, albeit long overdue, and Robinson had to be an exceptional man to make it work. The first few years weren't easy, but

more blacks followed, and many, like Robinson, were great players. It wasn't long before the majors were seeing the likes of Roy Campanella, Willie Mays, Roberto Clemente, Larry Doby, Monte Irvin, Ernie Banks and Henry Aaron.

Before 1947 blacks had had to play in separate negro leagues, and as a consequence many great baseball players never received the kind of recognition given their white counterparts. But Rickey and Robinson changed all that, and while those first years were rocky, baseball was the ultimate winner.

**Top:** L to R: Dodgers Joe Black, Duke Snider, manager Chuck Dressen, Pee Wee Reese, and Jackie Robinson celebrate a win during the '52 Series.

**Above:** Yankee heroes in game 5, '53 Series. Seated, L to R: Gil McDougald, Jim McDonald, Gene Woodling. Behind, Billy Martin, Mickey Mantle.

Just a few seasons after the "color line" had fallen baseball was once again able to really showcase its product. As the 1940s turned into the 1950s the team from the Bronx, the New York Yankees, again proved to be the game's most enduring dynasty. Making it even more interesting, the two greatest rivals to the American League Yanks were the National League Brooklyn Dodgers and New York Giants.

The Dodgers had their now-famed "Boys of Summer" lineup, with the likes of Robinson, Reese, Campanella, Snider, Hodges, Erskine, Roe, Newcombe, Furillo and Cox. The Giants offered the baseball world stars such as Mays, Thomson, Irvin, Maglie, Dark, Mueller, Stanky, Jansen, Lockman and Hearn. And the Yanks countered with DiMaggio, Mantle, Ford, Berra, Bauer, Woodling, Rizzuto, Martin, Henrich, Reynolds, Raschi and Lopat.

Even the managers had their own distinct personalities. There was Casey Stengel of the Yanks, the Old Perfesser, who could keep audiences entertained with his wit and wisdom, couched in a special kind of language dubbed "Stengelese" by the press. The Giants had Leo Durocher, Leo the Lip, a combative, aggressive skipper who would do anything to win. The Dodgers countered with wily Charlie Dressen, and later the quiet but effective Walter Alston.

It was a great time, and despite the calibre of the competition, the Yanks managed a record five straight pennants and World Series victories from 1949 to 1953. But there were other great teams and great players thrilling the fans in the 1950s. The Cleveland Indians had the big pitching staff, with Early Wynn, Bob Lemon, Mike Garcia and the aging Bob Feller. A few years later they would come up with a fireballing rookie lefthander named Herb Score.

The Detroit Tigers were showcasing a youngster named Al Kaline, the Pirates had Ralph Kiner and the Braves had Eddie Mathews and Warren Spahn to go along with young Henry Aaron. Cincinnati had big Ted Kluszewski and in 1956 came up with a remarkable rookie named Frank Robinson. Jackie Jensen was a top RBI man in Boston, playing alongside the still great Ted Williams. Young home run sluggers like Harmon Killebrew of Washington and Rocky Colavito of Cleveland also began banging down fences in the 1950s.

There were also more than enough outstanding pitchers during the 1950s. Robin Roberts was a perennial 20-game winner for the Phillies, Johnny Antonelli was solid with the Giants and Lew Burdette teamed with Spahn for the Braves. Besides the great Cleveland and Yankee staffs in the American League, the As had little Bobby Shantz, the Red Sox Mel Parnell, the Tigers Jim Bunning and Frank Lary and the Yanks Bob Turley.

Relief pitchers were also becoming stars in their own right for the first time. There was Jim Konstanty of the Phils, Hoyt Wilhelm of the Giants, Joe Black of the Dodgers, Don Mossi and Ray Narleski of Cleveland – just a few of many who became well known in the 1950s and set the stage for all who followed.

Records: there were plenty of those, perhaps the most famous being Don Larson's perfect

later a speedy shortstop, Maury Wills of the Dodgers, would steal 104 bases, erasing Ty Cobb's standard of 96 set way back in 1915.

The changing of the guard would also be marked by the retirements of Ted Williams and Stan Musial, and Warren Spahn, the winningest lefthander in the history of the game, was also nearing the end of the line. In 1964 the New York Yankees would win their fifth straight pennant, only to lose the Series to the St Louis Cardinals. It would be the last pennant for the Bronx Bombers for 12 years, marking the end of baseball's longest-running dynasty.

But some things never change. In 1941 the game's most dominant pitcher was a fireballing righthander named Bob Feller. In 1964 the game's most dominant pitcher was a fireballing lefthander named Sandy Koufax. The Dodger ace was just a year away from smashing Feller's single-season strikeout record of 348. He would whiff 382 in 1965.

In some ways there were more changes in baseball between 1941 and 1964 than in any other similar time period in the game's history. Baseball had weathered a world war, had broken its color line, had expanded to the West Coast, had seen great records broken and had introduced many great players. It was a time when there was something in the game for everyone, a time for all baseball fans to relish and remember, a Golden Age.

Let's take a closer look at it.

game for the Yanks against the Dodgers in the 1956 World Series. Ted Williams continued to make news, batting an incredible .388 at the advanced age of 39 in 1957, while a year earlier young Mickey Mantle had captured the fancy of the baseball world by winning the coveted triple crown. And there were many more great individual achievements.

But perhaps the biggest story of the 1950s was the spread of major league baseball to the West Coast, as both the Giants and Dodgers would leave New York after the 1957 season and take their franchises to San Francisco and Los Angeles respectively. That was something no one had anticipated a few years before.

The 1960s would see the beginning of still another great era in baseball. More young stars would come on the horizon, the game would expand by adding new teams, including a woeful bunch called the New York Mets, who lost 120 games in 1962 under a previously successful manager, Casey Stengel. There would also be some great records falling. In 1961 Roger Maris of the Yankees would blast 61 home runs, toppling the long-standing season record of 60 set by the immortal Babe Ruth in 1927. And a year

# CHAPTER I
# THE RECORD-SETTING SEASON

Indians ace Rapid Robert
Feller.

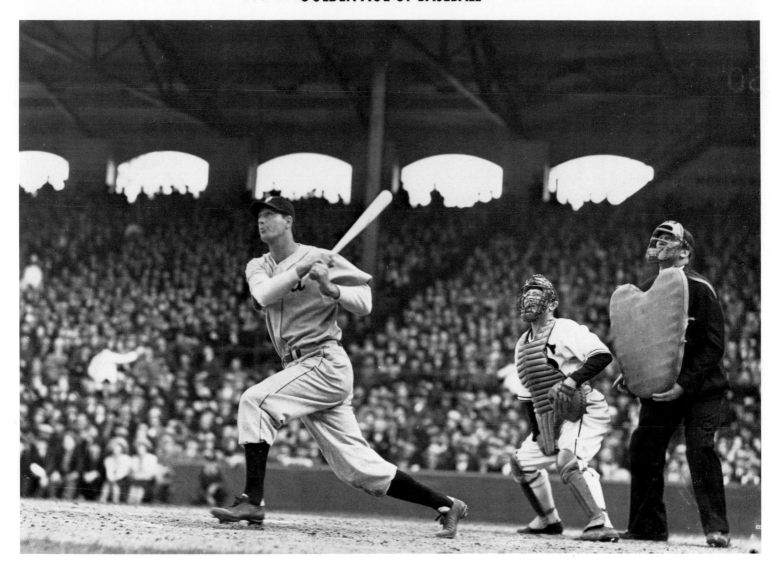

Major league baseball seemed to be on a high during the 1940 season. The sport was entering a new decade and that first year appeared to set the tone for what was to come. The American League set a new attendance record and the National wasn't far behind. Detroit and Cincinnati were the pennant winners that year, the Tigers topping the Indians by a game and the Yankees by two in a tight and exciting race. Cincy won the NL flag for the second straight year and emerged as the World Series champ in seven hard-fought games.

There were also enough exciting individual performances to help keep the fans hurrying through the turnstiles. It began on opening day when Cleveland's 21-year-old Bob Feller threw the first opening-day no-hitter in the history of the game. Detroit's Hank Greenberg belted 41 homers and drove home 150 runs that year, while Joe DiMaggio led the American League in hitting with a .352 batting average.

Big John Mize, with 43 homers and 137 ribbys, was becoming a major National League slugger, while Cincy's Frank McCormick, who led the NL in hits for a third straight year, was the league's Most Valuable Player. Both the Dodgers and Cardinals were building fine teams

to challenge the Reds, and there was no reason to believe that 1941 wouldn't be an even greater season in both leagues.

It was left to those who looked past the confines of the diamond to the rising war clouds in Europe to wonder what would happen to the game should the United States be drawn into the ever-widening European conflict. But the possibility of war wasn't really on the minds of baseball fans as the new season began. They were more interested in the Yankees and the Dodgers, in Williams, DiMaggio, Mize and Feller, and in an exciting Brooklyn rookie named Pete Reiser, a speedy switch-hitting outfielder who seemed able to do it all.

The Yanks quickly established themselves as the class of the American League. Besides DiMaggio, the Bronx Bombers featured outfielders Tommy Henrich and Charley "King Kong" Keller, infielders Joe Gordon, Phil Rizzuto and Red Rolfe, catcher Bill Dickey and pitchers Red Ruffing, Spud Chandler and Johnny Murphy. As the season wore on the Yanks would make a shambles of the AL race.

In the senior circuit a two-team race developed between the Dodgers and St Louis Cardinals, a seesaw chase that would see the lead change

**Above:** Hall of Fame slugger Hank Greenberg hits another.

**Opposite above:** Big John Mize could hit the ball out of any ballpark.

**Opposite below:** The Yankee Clipper, Joe DiMaggio.

some 27 times during the season. And while the Yanks would clinch the pennant on 4 September, the earliest clinching to that time, the Dodgers would go nearly to the wire before edging the Cards by a scant 2½ games.

But before the season would end, the pennant races would take a back seat to a number of individual events, especially in the American League. The first involved none other than Joe DiMaggio, the Yankee Clipper.

DiMag was coming off two straight American League batting titles when 1941 began, but he, like the Yankees, started slowly. In mid-May the Clipper was fighting a slump, and the Bronx Bombers were a .500 team, already trailing Cleveland by 5½ games. On 15 May the club lost another one, this time to the White Sox, but DiMaggio contributed a run-scoring single off Edgar Smith. Very few people read anything into the hit except that maybe the Clipper's bat was finally going to come alive.

Come alive it did, and in a way no major leaguer's bat had ever come alive before or since. For Joe DiMaggio was about to embark on a hitting streak that would last some two months. During all that time DiMag would get at least one hit per ballgame, setting a record that stands

to this day, a record many baseball people feel will never be broken.

Like most streaks, there wasn't much attention paid until it reached 30 games. That's when he broke the Yankee club record and the watch began in earnest. Against the St Louis Browns in the 36th game DiMag got a basehit in his final at bat in the eighth inning. Two games later submariner Elden Auker had the Clipper taking the collar until the eighth. The Yanks were leading and this would undoubtedly be their final at bat.

DiMag came up with two out and promptly smashed a double over third base to keep the streak alive. On 29 June the Clipper hit in his 42nd straight game, to break the American League record set by the great George Sisler in 1922. Then, three games later, he broke Wee Willie Keeler's all-time mark of 44 straight, established way back in 1897. Joe D was now the record holder all by himself, and the question was how high could he go?

He took the record past 50 games, and by that time baseball fans everywhere were watching. For awhile it looked as if it would never end. Six times during the streak DiMag faced a now-or-never situation in his final at bat, and six times he came through with hits.

The streak stood at 56 games when the Yanks had a 17 July date with the Cleveland Indians at Municipal Stadium. With some 40,000 fans in attendance, Joe and the Yankees went up against Cleveland lefthander Al Smith. In his first two times up DiMag hit a pair of hot smashes toward third. Each looked like a sure hit, but both times Cleveland third-sacker Ken Keltner came up with a great play to throw Joe out. The third time up he walked, and when he came up for perhaps

the final time in the eighth, he was facing righty Jim Bagby, Jr.

Again Joe hit the ball hard. But this one was grabbed by shortstop Lou Boudreau, who turned the shot into a double play. That was it. The streak had ended, but Joe DiMaggio had made baseball history. In addition, he had lit a fire under his teammates, who won 41 of the 56 games in which he hit safely, putting them solidly back in first place.

During his amazing streak Joe D had 91 hits in 223 at bats for a .408 mark. He banged out 16 doubles, four triples, 15 home runs and drove home 55 runs. He was also walked 21 times and struck out on just seven occasions. And to further show his greatness, after being shut out at Cleveland, the Yankee clipper went out the next day and promptly started a 17-game hit streak. As Hall of Famer George Sisler said when the Clipper passed his old mark of 41 straight, "The guy is a natural in everything he does and is a great hitter. His streak is no lucky fluke, believe me."

DiMaggio's streak had drawn so much attention during its duration that very few people noticed another American League star creating some hitting excitement of his own. Ted Williams, the Boston Red Sox' "Splendid Splinter," was batting over .400 for the season. In fact, while DiMaggio was hitting .408 during his 56-game streak, Williams was batting .412. But once the DiMaggio streak ended and it became obvious that the Yanks had the AL flag wrapped up, all eyes turned toward Williams.

Williams had been a great hitter ever since joining the Sox as a rookie in 1939. He played in 149 games that year, hitting .327, with 31 homers

**Above:** Joe DiMaggio gets another hit in his 56-game streak in 1941.

**Opposite top:** Basehits were routine for Ted Williams, the major leagues' last .400 hitter, in 1941.

**Opposite far right:** With batting callouses on both hands, Di-Mag acknowledges the end of his great hitting streak after he was blanked at Cleveland on July 18, 1941.

**Opposite right:** Joe D's teammates help celebrate during the greatest hitting streak of all-time.

and a rookie record of 145 runs batted in. Two years later he was attempting to become the major leagues' first .400 hitter since Bill Terry had topped the coveted mark in 1930. Many felt the .400 hitter was a thing of the past, and indeed after 1941 he would be. But Williams wasn't about to surrender to the odds without a fight.

By mid-September, the Splinter was hitting .413, and it looked as if he might make it. But with the pressure mounting, Ted's average began to dip. Coming into a season-ending doubleheader at Philadelphia, his average was officially listed at .399955. Red Sox manager Joe Cronin knew the kind of pressure Williams was under. He also knew that a .399955 average would go in the books as .400. So he told his young outfielder that he could sit out the twin bill and not risk losing his .400 mark. But to Williams, the competitor, .399955 was not .400, and the Splinter calmly told his manager, "I don't want to hit .400 by my shirttails."

So Williams went out to face righthander Dick Fowler. And when he came up to hit for the first time, Athletics' catcher Frank Hayes wished him luck, then added: "We're not giving you a damn thing, Ted. Mr Mack [Manager Connie Mack] told us if we let up on you he'll run us out of baseball."

That was the only way Williams would have wanted it. He wasted no time in picking out a Fowler pitch and lining it for a basehit. Next time up he did even better: he belted a long home run over the rightfield fence. He was over .400 now without a doubt and could have left the game then and there, but he didn't. Facing lefty Porter Vaughn the next two times up he again whacked solid singles.

**Left:** By mid-August, 1941, Williams was batting .410. Ted ended the season with a .406 mark.

With four hits in the first game he could easily have sat down for the second. But once again he insisted on playing, and this time he got a double and single in four trips. Under the greatest of pressure, Williams had gone six for eight in the doubleheader and finished the season with nothing in doubt. His final batting average was .406.

While many eyes were focused on the American League and their record-breaking players, the Dodgers were winning a tight National League race. The Brooks had a pair of 22-game winners in Whitlow Wyatt and Kirby Higbe, the home run and RBI leader in Dolph Camilli, with 34 and 120, as well as the batting champion in rookie of the year Pete Reiser, who hit a solid .343. In addition to the batting title, Reiser led the senior circuit in slugging, runs, doubles and triples.

Still, the Yankees were heavy favorites when the World Series began. Joe McCarthy was piloting the Yanks, and he had already led the Bombers to five Series triumphs. Leo Durocher was the Dodger skipper that year, and he had helped the Brooklyn team to its first pennant in 21 years. He was a man who hated to lose.

But though Leo the Lip didn't like to lose, the seasoned Yankees knew how to win. They took the opening game at Yankee Stadium 3-2 behind righthander Red Ruffing. Wyatt got the Dodgers

**Above:** Rival managers in the 1941 Series: the Yanks' Joe McCarthy and the Dodgers' Leo Durocher.

even by an identical score in game two, and returning to the friendly confines of Ebbets Field in Brooklyn, Durocher's ballclub felt it was in good shape.

But Marius Russo threw a four-hitter for the Yanks in game three, as the Bombers bunched together four singles in the eighth inning off reliever Hugh Casey to take a 2-1 victory. Then, in game four, there occurred one of the best-remembered plays in World Series history.

The Dodgers had a 4-3 lead going into the ninth inning. They were three outs away from tying the Series once more. Moments later they were just an out away, as reliever Casey faced Yankee rightfielder Tommy Henrich. With two strikes, Casey broke off a big curve and Henrich swung . . . and missed!

Dodger fans roared. For a split second they thought they had won it, until they saw the ball squirting away from catcher Mickey Owen. He had dropped the third strike, and Henrich scampered safely to first base. So the Yanks had a second chance, and they made the most of it. DiMaggio singled, Charley Keller smacked a double, Bill Dickey walked and Joe Gordon followed with another double. Presto! just like that the Yankees had four runs and went on to win the game 7-4. All because of a dropped third strike.

The next day Ernie Bonham four-hit the Dodgers, and the Yanks wrapped up the 1941 World Series with a 3-1 triumph. So ended the last season that would be completely normal for the next five years.

Even though the United States was not officially involved in the World War during the 1941 season, the war's presence was already being felt in major league baseball. The Detroit Tigers' slugging star, Hank Greenberg, who had been starring in the American League since 1934 and was at the peak of his career, was the first big star to be affected.

Greenberg was coming off a great 1940 season in which he had batted .340 and was leading the league in homers, with 41, and RBIs, with 150. But when selective service, the military draft, was begun in the fall of 1940, Greenberg drew a very low draft number. No one thought much about it until May 1941 when, after playing just 19 games, the man who had hit 58 home runs in 1938 was drafted into the army. At the time, Greenberg was 30 years old and the highest-paid player in the major leagues. Yet he left the game immediately and became a humble private in the army. He would miss the rest of the season and nearly four more years after that.

Ironically, in December 1941 the US government put into effect a new rule that permitted the armed services to discharge all men over the age of 28. On 5 December Hank Greenberg left the service. Two days later the Japanese attacked Pearl Harbor, and America was at war. Greenberg immediately re-enlisted, this time opting for officer candidates' school.

Within two years almost all of baseball's major stars would also be gone, and the game itself would be nearing collapse.

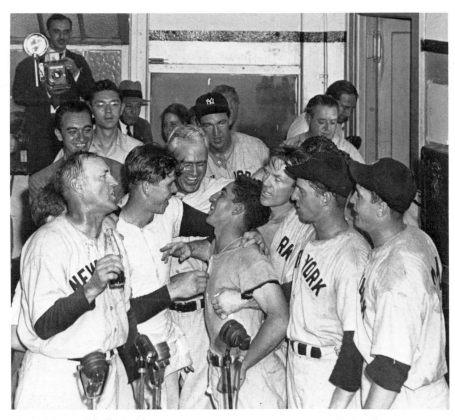

**Above:** The Yanks celebrate after winning the '41 World Series. In the middle of the crowd is shortstop Phil Rizzuto.

**Right:** Dodger catcher Mickey Owen drops a third strike to Tommy Henrich during the '41 Series. The gaff allowed the Yanks to win game.

**Opposite above:** The Yanks' Charley Keller slides safely into third during 1941 Series action. A wild pitch will bring him home.

**Right:** Hank Greenberg was one of the first big stars to enter military service in early 1942.

# CHAPTER II
# THE
# WAR YEARS

Ted Williams being sworn in as Naval Aviation Cadet in May of 1942.

**Above:** Longtime Commissioner of Baseball Kenesaw Mountain Landis.

**Middle below:** Twilight baseball at Brooklyn's Ebbets Field began in June of 1942.

It wasn't long after the Japanese attack on Pearl Harbor that baseball players began enlisting. Like all other Americans, they knew the war was going to be long and difficult. There was no way ballplayers could, or wanted to, receive special treatment, not with a world war beginning to rage on two fronts, and before the 1942 season got underway many people began to wonder if the game would even continue.

Baseball Commissioner Kenesaw Mountain Landis, who had ruled over the game with an iron hand since 1921, wanted to know that too. Not wishing to start the 1942 season only to have it stopped again, Judge Landis decided to go right to the source. He wrote a letter to President Franklin D Roosevelt which said in part:

"Baseball is about to adopt schedules, sign players, make vast commitments, go to training camps. What do you want it to do? If you believe we ought to close down for the duration of the war, we are ready to do so immediately. If you feel we ought to continue, we would be delighted to do so. We await your order."

The President wasted no time in giving the Commissioner his answer. He felt that baseball was an important part of American life and therefore should continue.

"I honestly feel that it would be best for the country to keep baseball going," he wrote. "There will be fewer people unemployed and everybody will work longer hours and harder than ever before. And that means that they ought to have a chance for recreation and for taking their minds off their work even more than before."

That was the final word. Baseball would continue, but in what form? Before the war would end in 1945 some 500 major leaguers would be pressed into service, not to mention the hundreds of others whose absence stripped the minor leagues of much of its stockpiled talent. In

fact, during the course of the conflict, some 32 minor league ballclubs *were* forced to suspend operations. Others began recruiting veteran players, some long retired, or raw teenagers to fill their rosters.

On the other hand, while many of the major leaguers in the service saw war action, others spent a good deal of time playing ball for military teams. There was a game in Cleveland between Army and Navy teams just before the 1942 All-Star Game that drew more than 62,000 fans. Many of those Clevelanders in attendance wanted to see their ace pitcher, Bob Feller, who was slated to star for Mickey Cochrane's Great Lakes Naval Training Station team.

But what about the regular season? Since the ballplayers didn't all leave at once, 1942 wasn't a bad year. Indeed, it was an outstanding year for many players. Ted Williams, who would eventually serve in both World War II and the Korean conflict of the early 1950s, was able to complete the 1942 season before entering the service, and all the Splendid Splinter did that year was win the American League triple crown with a .356 batting average, 36 home runs and 137 runs batted in.

The National League might have had a record-breaker of its own that year. The Dodgers' Pistol Pete Reiser, in just his second full season, was living up to all the predictions and putting together some great numbers. By July Reiser was hitting close to .390, and there was even talk of a .400 season. But this man who

played the game with such reckless abandon was also about to pay the price.

It happened in St Louis. Reiser was chasing a long fly when he ran smack into the centerfield fence at full speed. The result was a severe concussion, but being a hell-for-leather competitor, Reiser came back too soon and tried to play through the headaches and dizzy spells. By season's end his average was down to .310.

In fact, whenever Reiser began playing well again it seemed he would run into another wall. It was a habit he couldn't shake. During the course of his career he had a pair of broken ankles, a severe knee injury, a broken elbow, torn muscles in his leg and several more concussions. Outfield fences, it seems, were Pete Reiser's own personal Pearl Harbors.

Reiser's injury also slowed the Dodger express that year, and that was certainly one of several factors that enabled the Cards to take the National League pennant by two games. St Louis, under the leadership of general manager Branch Rickey, had built another fine team. They had a pair of 20-game winners in Mort Cooper and Johnny Beazley, the only senior circuit hurlers to win 20 that year. The team also featured graceful Marty Marion at shortstop, Walker Cooper behind the plate and a super outfield of Enos Slaughter, Terry Moore and a rookie named Stan Musial. It was a solid Cardinal team that would, despite the war, win four National League pennants in five years. And Musial, a converted pitcher who hit .315 in 1942, would become the league's best hitter for nearly

**Below left:** Bob Feller (l.) and Walker Cooper were teammates in the service.

**Below:** Pistol Pete Reiser had his career shortened by injuries.

two decades. Yet as good as they were, the Cards were underdogs when the 1942 World Series rolled around because they were facing the mighty New York Yankees. The Bronx Bombers had won their sixth pennant in seven years and had their usual cast of star players.

Though the Cards had won 106 regular season games, compared to 103 for the Bombers, the New Yorkers had lost only four games in all their five previous World Series victories since 1936! And when the Bombers won the opening tilt in St Louis 7-4, with Red Ruffing besting Mort Cooper, it looked as though the Yanks were on their way once again.

But then things turned around, and in rather dramatic fashion. The Cards had scored all four of their first-game runs in the ninth inning, and now they got a pair in the first frame of game two. From there they went on to take a 4-3 victory behind Beazley, getting the winning tally in the bottom of the eighth on a triple by Whitey Kurowsky. In game three, played at Yankee Stadium, southpaw Ernie White tossed a six-hit shutout, and the Cards suddenly had a 2-1 lead.

A day later the Cardinals showed it was no fluke, this time outslugging the Bombers 9-6 and getting 12 hits along the way. And the next afternoon Johnny Beazley won his second game, clinching the Series with a 4-2 victory over the Yanks and Red Ruffing. It was a surprising and exciting end to a season that many people had thought might not even be played.

But still the list of top players leaving for the armed forces continued to grow. The Dodgers lost their fine shortstop, Pee Wee Reese, as well as the injury-prone Reiser, while the defending-champion Cards would be without pitcher Beazley and outfielder Moore. The Yanks had already lost old reliable Tommy Henrich in 1942, and the following year saw DiMaggio, Phil Rizzuto and Red Ruffing go to work for Uncle Sam. By the beginning of 1944 nearly 60 percent of the major league ballplayers were wearing another kind of uniform.

The Yanks and Cards repeated their pennant-winning performances in 1943. Young Stan Musial was a one-man wrecking crew for St Louis, leading the league in hitting, with a .357 mark, and also topping the NL, with 220 hits, 48 doubles, 20 triples, 347 total bases and a .562 slugging percentage. Mort Cooper won another 21 games, while Bill Nicholson of the Cubs led the league in homers, with 29, and runs batted in, with 128.

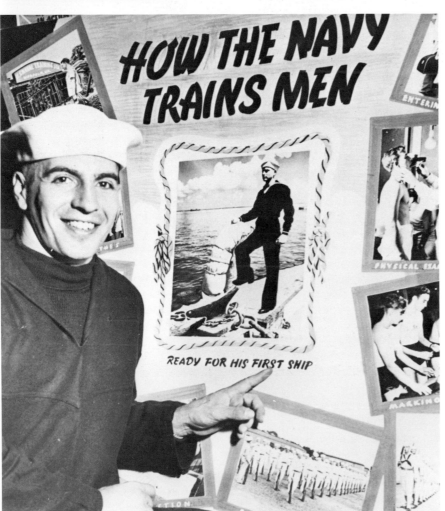

**Top left:** Stan "The Man" Musial in 1943.

**Left:** Phil Rizzuto as a Navy seaman in October, 1942.

Luke Appling of the White Sox, who had batted .388 back in 1936, took the American League batting title, with a .328 mark, while Rudy York of Detroit topped the junior circuit in homers and RBIs, netting 34 and 118 respectively. But there was little doubt that the quality of play was being affected by the war.

The World Series of 1943 opened in Yankee Stadium, where, due to wartime travel restrictions, the first three games would be played. The New Yorkers again won game one, this time riding home on the strong arm of Spud Chandler for a 4-2 victory. But when the Cooper brothers, pitcher Mort and catcher Walker, led the Cards to a 4-3 win in game two, despite the death of their father that very morning, St Louis fans began hoping for a repeat of 1942. Only this time it wasn't to be. The Yankees swept the next three by scores of 6-2, 2-1 and 2-0, Marius Russo and Spud Chandler pitching brilliantly in the final two games, to give the Bronx Bombers yet another world title.

In 1944 the national pastime would really feel the full affects of the worldwide conflict. It was a year in which a 15-year-old pitcher would hurl

for the Cincinnati Reds and a 16-year-old would play shortstop for the Brooklyn Dodgers. It was also a year in which a 40-year-old rookie would appear in the Detroit Tigers lineup and a 40-year-old veteran would return to the game after a four-year absence to help out the St Louis Cardinals. in their time of need.

**Top:** DiMaggio, Slaughter, Keller, Moore in 1942.

**Above:** Rizzuto stealing.

That's not the kind of stuff the major leagues were normally made of, but the increasing dearth of talent called for drastic measures. There were nearly 200 players in the majors by 1944 and 1945 who had enough physical ailments to be classified 4-F by their local draft boards. Yet they were sound enough to become big league ballplayers during the last years of the war.

Virtually every team had been weakened considerably by the loss of players when the 1944 season began. The Yankees were once again in the thick of the American League race, but now they were being challenged by an unlikely club.

Led by Vern Stephens and Mike Kreevich, as well as by pitchers Nelson Potter and Jack Kramer, the St Louis Browns were keeping pace with the Yanks. The Browns had never won a pennant in the long history of the franchise, and many thought they never would.

Over in the National League the Cards still had enough talent to take their third straight pennant. Led by the hitting of Stan Musial, who batted .347, and the pitching of 22-game winner Mort Cooper, the Cards were never seriously challenged. Their shortstop, Marty Marion, followed Cooper and Musial as the league's Most

**Below:** A US Air Force B-17 Flying Fortress bomber buzzed Yankee Stadium during the opener of the '43 World Series.

Valuable Player. And when the St Louis Browns edged the Yanks on the last day of the season, it set up a unique World Series, one of the few times both pennant winning teams played at the same ballpark.

Sportsman's Park in St Louis was the scene of the 1944 fall classic, and it was the Cardinals who again became world champions in six games. Musial and Walker Cooper were the Cards' top hitters, while four different pitchers won a game apiece. The Browns hit just .183 as a team, negating a strong effort by their pitchers. It would be the only pennant the old Brownies

would win in their history. The franchise would move to Baltimore in 1954, where it would achieve considerably more success.

But the World Series was not the big baseball story in 1944. Rather, it was some of the strange things that began to happen because of the increasingly debilitating effects of the war. For example, with Pee Wee Reese, the great Dodger shortstop, in the service, Brooklyn brought up a kid named Tommy Brown to fill in. Brown, a Brooklyn native, was born on 6 December 1927, so when he played 46 games in 1944, batting .164, he was just 16 years old.

**Left:** The Yanks' Spud Chandler won two games in the '43 Series.

**Bottom:** Three former big league stars in the Pacific. L to r: Big Jim Bivin, Long Tom Winsett and Preacher Dorsett.

To his credit, Brown was not just a one-year wonder. Though never a star, he remained with the Dodgers as a utility player until 1951, then played the last two years of his career with Philadelphia and Chicago. His lifetime batting average was just .241, but he batted .303 in 41 games for the Dodgers in 1949 and .320 for the Cubs in 61 games in 1952. Had it not been for the war, Tommy Brown would have undoubtedly have spent a few more years in the minors and perhaps have been, in the long run, a better big league player.

Brown wasn't the only kid player. Like many other ballclubs, the 1944 Cincinnati Reds were short of pitchers. They began looking around and suddenly came up with a find. He was a left-handed pitcher from nearby Hamilton, Ohio, a high school phenom who seemed to have a world of stuff. So the Reds not only signed 15-year-old Joe Nuxhall, they brought him up to the majors, and when he got into a ballgame he became the youngest player ever to appear in the big leagues.

Nuxhall, of course, wasn't ready for the big time and he got tattooed in his first and only outing of the year. To show the folly of bringing up a 15-year-old kid, it took Joe Nuxhall eight more years to return to the majors. He then pitched from 1952 to 1966, putting together a respectable career that saw him win 135 ballgames. But in 1944 the Reds had no business rushing him up to the majors.

And what about Chuck Hostetler? That's an obscure name that even the most rabid of baseball fans or trivia buffs might not recognize. Charles Cloyd Hostetler was purely a product of the war years. He was an outfielder who came up to the Detroit Tigers in 1944, playing in 90 games and hitting a respectable .298. What was

unusual about him was that rookie Hostetler was 40 years old when he joined the Tigers, having been born in 1903. He even returned the next year, hitting only .159 in 42 games, but as soon as the war ended, and the players began returning from service, Hostetler and many others were gone.

During the off-season another baseball era came to an end, though this had nothing to do with the still-raging war. Judge Kenesaw Mountain Landis, baseball's first and only commissioner, died on 25 November 1944 at the age of 78. Judge Landis had been the commissioner since early in 1921 and had helped restore baseball to a position of respectability following the disastrous Black Sox Scandal. By banning the eight members of the Chicago White Sox for life after they had allegedly conspired with gamblers to fix the 1919 World Series (they had previously been acquitted in a civil trial), Judge Landis quickly showed he was going to be a strong and responsible ruler. And he remained that until his death.

The new Commissioner would be AB "Happy" Chandler, a former Governor and US Senator from Kentucky, who would spend only seven years in the same office that Judge Landis had occupied for more than 20 years. But Chandler was the Commissioner during one of the most important events in baseball and sports history. And when he took office that event was just a few years away. But first he had to help see baseball through the conclusion of the war, which seemed close to ending as the 1945 season got under way. That, however, didn't help the quality of play or some of the strange roster moves dictated by the need to find players.

It was a year in which big league teams would

make nearly 1500 more errors than usual, once again showing the deteriorating quality of play. But while attendance had been down the past two seasons, it began picking up again in 1945, especially in the final months, when the war had ended and the star players began to return.

At the beginning of the season, though, the teams were still scrambling. The Dodgers, for instance, signed outfielder Floyd "Babe" Herman in 1945. Back in 1930 Herman had batted .393 for the Brooks, and the year before hit .381. In fact, he was a lifetime .300 hitter, with a career mark over .320. So what was the catch? Only this. Babe Herman had retired from baseball in 1937 and had been out of the game for some eight years when the Dodgers brought him back. He was 42 years old, yet still played in 37 games and hit .265. So he contributed. The next year, of course, he, too, was gone.

Stranger still was the case of Paul Schreiber, who was born on 8 October 1902. At the age of 19 Schreiber had pitched a single game for the Brooklyn Dodgers. That was in 1922. The next year he appeared in nine games for the Dodgers and had no decisions. After that he left the active roster, remaining merely a part-time batting practice pitcher for the next 22 years. Yet in 1945, lo and behold, the Yankees signed him to pitch. He pitched in just two games and once again had no decisions.

There was more. A former big league pitcher named Charles "Red" Lucas, who had won 157 games between 1923 and 1938, came out of retirement to be a pinch hitter for Nashville of the Southern Association. At age 43 Lucas showed the kids how it was done, banging the ball at a .421 clip.

There are similar examples, but perhaps the most famous, and perhaps most unusual as well, was the case of Pete Gray. In 1944 outfielder Gray was playing for Nashville in the Southern Association and putting together a great season. He batted .333, hit five home runs and swiped 68 bases. For his efforts Gray was named the Southern Association's Most Valuable Player. But what really made the story amazing was the fact that Pete Gray only had one arm!

Gray had lost his right arm in a truck accident some years before, yet continued his pursuit of a baseball career. And he quickly compensated for his handicap. Though not a big man, he was able to whip the bat around with one arm and even generate occasional home run power. When he

**Top left:** Joe Nuxhall, shown here later in his career, first pitched for the Reds at age 15 in 1945, the result of a wartime shortage of players.

**Top:** The St Louis Browns signed outfielder Pete Gray in 1945, despite the fact that he had only one arm. Gray played in 77 games and batted .218 that year.

**Left:** American soldiers make time for a baseball game during the campaign in Luxembourg in 1943.

**Right:** Yankee Manager Joe McCarthy chats with some wounded soldiers visiting the Yank training camp at Atlantic City in March of 1945.

caught a ball or picked up a basehit in the field, he had to toss the ball in the air, discard his glove, then catch the ball in his now-bared hand before making the throw.

Showing guts and determination, Gray came up to the St Louis Browns in 1945 and played in 61 big league ballgames. He hit just .218, but considering his handicap it was still quite an achievement. Like many others who got their chance because of all the missing players, Gray was gone when the 1946 season began. But his courage and ability would become the subject of a full length television movie more than 40 years later.

Not to be left out of the act, the Washington Senators also gave a handicapped player a chance. His name was Bert Shepard, a left-handed pitcher who was intent on making it to the bigs before going into military service. But during the war Shepard's plane was shot down and he lost his right leg just below the knee. Out of the service, Shepard was fitted with a wooden leg, and he began pitching again, harboring an almost impossible dream.

Finally the old Senators gave Shepard his chance. They signed him to a contract and put him into a game against the Boston Red Sox. Shepard actually went five and one-third innings, giving up just one run on three hits and striking out a pair of Bosox. Not a bad debut, but

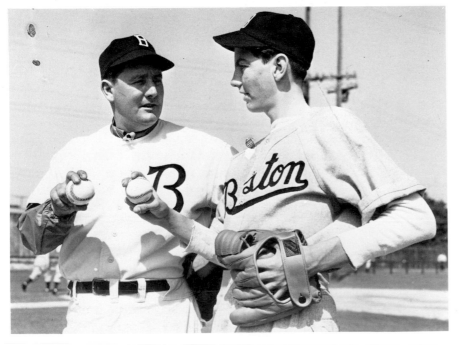

that was it. Shepard had realized his dream, and the Senators decided not to take any further chances. He never pitched in a big league game again.

What about the pennant races of 1945? They were there, but they were also affected by the loss of personnel. In fact, even the All-Star Game was cancelled in 1945, the only time the mid-season classic has been called off since its inception in 1933. The reason given was wartime travel restrictions, but most fans felt it was because there were just too few genuine stars to put a game together.

In the National League the Cardinals were hurt by the loss of Stan Musial to the Navy and by the trade of Mort Cooper to Boston. That was just enough to take the winning edge away, and the Chicago Cubs, led by their first baseman, Phil Cavaretta, ascended to the crown. Cavaretta batted .355, to win the batting title and then the MVP prize.

Tommy Holmes of Boston led the league in home runs, with 28, but that wasn't the only news Holmes made. The Braves outfielder compiled a 37-game hitting streak from 6 June to 8 July, establishing a new National League record. With the help of the streak, Holmes batted .352 for the season, a career best. The RBI leader was Dixie Walker of the Dodgers, while Red Barrett, Hank Wyse and Hank Borowy were the senior circuit's 20 game winners, none of them exactly household names.

In the American League the Detroit Tigers were in a three-way fight with Washington and St Louis. The Tigers got a giant shot in the arm on 1 July, when Hank Greenberg returned to the team. Greenberg had been one of the first superstars to join the war effort, and now he was one of the first to return. In his first game back the man who had once clubbed 58 home runs hit a round-tripper to celebrate his return and help his club defeat the As 9-5, while some 48,000 fans at Briggs Stadium screamed in approval.

It didn't take Greenberg long to regain his batting eye. Without him the Tigers undoubtedly would have finished second to the Washington Senators. As it turned out, the race was decided on the final day of the season, when the Tigers met the 1944 champs, the St Louis Browns, on a rainy field in St Louis. If St Louis won, Detroit would be forced into a playoff with Washington. Going into the ninth inning of the crucial game the Browns had a 3-2 lead, and the Tigers were down to their last three outs.

With Nelson Potter on the mound for St Louis, pinch hitter Hub Walker singled. Skeeter Webb then bunted, and Browns' first baseman George McQuinn tried to get Walker at second, but the throw was late. With first base open, St

**Opposite top:** Dixie Walker, known as the "People's Cherce" in Brooklyn, was a fine Dodger hitter in the mid-1940s.

**Opposite bottom:** Mort Cooper of the Braves shows finer points of pitching to his younger brother, Sam, in 1946.

**Top:** Hank Greenberg returned from the service to hit more home runs for the Tigers.

**Above:** The Yanks' George Stirnweiss heads for home as Rick Ferrell of the Senators gets set to make the tag.

Louis manager Luke Sewell ordered Doc Creamer walked, loading the bases.

That brought up Greenberg. And in a story-book ending the big slugger parked one, a grand slam home run that brought a pennant to Detroit and perhaps symbolically brought an end to what had been the war years in the major leagues. After missing nearly four and a half peak years to the military, Hank Greenberg had returned to hit 13 homers, bat .311 and drive in 60 runs in just 78 games.

Greenberg wasn't a one-man show. Left-hander Hal Newhouser won 25 games and Rudy York contributed a big clutch bat. Yet some of the other American League leaders clearly showed the lingering affects of the war.

George "Snuffy" Stirnweiss of the Yankees was the American League batting champion, with a .309 average. In fact, Stirnweiss had hit .319 in 154 games the year before. Yet in 1946, with all the veterans back, he hit just .251 and would never hit above .261 again. In addition, Stirnweiss belted 10 home runs to go with his batting title in 1945. He would hit only 10 home runs total during the next seven seasons.

One final testimony to the overall lack of strength in the American League during the last two years of the war: the second- and third-place finishers in the American League batting race in 1945 were Tony Cuccinello and John Dickshot, both of them White Sox, who hit .308 and .302

**Above:** This group of happy Detroit Tigers just won the 1945 World Series. L to R are Art Houtteman, Skeeter Webb, Hal Newhouser and Bob Maier.

**Right:** First baseman Phil Cavaretta of the Cubs led his team to a pennant in 1945, hitting .355 and taking home the National League's MVP prize.

respectively. With the veterans back the following year, both players were released and never appeared in the major leagues again.

Despite everything, there was still a World Series in 1945, the Tigers going up against the Cubs. And in the first game at Detroit the Chicagoans showed they meant business. They not only roughed up Tiger ace Hal Newhouser, but got a masterly pitching performance from Hank Borowy and won the game 9-0, with Phil Cavaretta and Andy Pafka both getting three hits.

In game two the Tigers pitched Virgil "Fire" Trucks, who had rejoined the team from the armed forces at the end of the regular season. Trucks pitched a fine game, and Detroit won 4-1, getting all of their runs in the fifth inning, the final three riding home on a Greenberg homer. Then, in game three at Wrigley Field in Chicago, the Cubs' Claude Passeau, a 17-game winner during the regular season, pitched a fine one-hitter, winning 3-0 and putting Chicago back on top by a game.

The seesaw continued, and baseball fans found they were seeing an exciting World Series.

Dizzy Trout of the Tigers was a 4-1 winner in game four, and in the fifth contest Newhouser pitched Detroit into a 3-2 game lead, 8-4.

Game six was a real cliffhanger. The Cubs had a 5-1 lead after five and a 7-3 advantage at the end of six. But the Tigers came roaring back. Detroit struck for four runs in the top of the seventh to tie the game. Then it remained scoreless into the bottom of the 12th. Dizzy Trout was back on the mound for the Tigers when the Cubs put Bill Schuster on first. Stan Hack then smacked what looked like a single to left. But the ball suddenly took a bad hop right over Hank Greenberg's shoulder, and Schuster came all the way around to score the winning run and force a seventh and deciding game.

Detroit had Hal Newhouser ready to go, while Chicago gambled on Hank Borowy, who had pitched four shutout innings in the sixth game two days earlier. The gamble failed. Borowy didn't retire a single batter, and before the first inning ended the Tigers had five runs. From then on they coasted behind Newhouser to a 9-3 victory and a world championship.

Phil Cavaretta had lived up to his MVP season, with 11 hits and a .423 average in the Series, while Greenberg was the top power man, with two homers, three doubles, seven RBIs and a .304 average. After being roughed up in game one, Newhouser pitched two fine ballgames and fanned 22 Cubs in 20 and two-thirds innings of work. The seven-game Series was a fitting climax to the season and also officially signified the end of baseball's war years.

The 1946 season would mark a return to normalcy. Attendance would boom in both leagues, and baseball would have all its stars back. DiMaggio, Feller, Musial and Willians would once again electrify the fans. But the game wouldn't be free of controversy, either. There would be the outlawed Mexican League, trying to tempt players to jump south of the border. And Branch Rickey, the general manager of the Brooklyn Dodgers, would test the game in a way it had never been tested before. He would sign a player named Jackie Robinson and attempt to make him the first black man ever to play in the major leagues.

**Above:** Southpaw Hal Newhouser fires one to the Cubs' Frank Secory during 7th-game action in the 1945 World Series. Prince Hal pitched his team to a 9-3 victory in the finale.

# CHAPTER III
# THE COLOR LINE

A young Jackie Robinson in the uniform of the Kansas City Monarchs.

**Right:** Branch Rickey was one of baseball's great innovators and the man who decided that it was time for the "color line" to be erased.

**Far right:** Adrian "Cap" Anson, posing here in later years, was a Hall of Fame player in the 19th century and also one of the prime movers in keeping blacks out of big league baseball.

**Below right:** Black second-baseman Charlie Grant. He almost had a shot at the majors in 1901. But that was because John McGraw was going to pass him off as a full-blooded Indian.

The timing was interesting. In August 1945 the second war to end all wars came to a close. For the first time in four years baseball would be returning to normal – at least that's what fans, players and baseball executives hoped. By 1946 the hundreds of players, including nearly all the game's superstars, would be returning to the fold. And with the tension of the war past, travel restrictions lifted and the country in a festive mood, there was no reason to believe that attendance wouldn't soar.

While all this was happening, one of baseball's great innovators was putting his own private plan into action, a plan that he knew might possibly cause a widespread upheaval within the game, but one that would eventually change the entire face of the national pastime. The innovator's name was Branch Rickey, and he was one of the most successful baseball executives of his time. Often called the father of the modern farm system, Rickey was the first man to see the benefit of a club developing its own talent through a well organized system of minor league teams. He first worked his farm system magic in St Louis, where he developed a deep and talented Cardinal team that would win four pennants in five years during the 1940s. But Rickey was eased out of his job with the Cards after the 1942 season, and he was subsequently hired by Brooklyn, where he became the Dodgers' team president and, in effect, general manager.

Rickey wanted to duplicate his St Louis success in Brooklyn, but he wanted to do it in a different kind of way. It was no secret that there was a very large number of talented black baseball players. There always had been. The problem was that no black man had been allowed to play in the major leagues in the 20th century. Branch Rickey felt that this was an injustice that had to be dealt with. He also felt that if he were the first to begin stockpiling black talent, and then bring the players to the majors, he could build a very powerful baseball team in Brooklyn.

But could it be done? There had not been a black in major league baseball since before the turn of the century, if then. The history books generally agree that two brothers, Welday and Moses Walker, who played for Toledo of the American Association in 1884, came the closest, for many then thought Toledo big league.

It is also generally agreed that perhaps the man most responsible for drawing the now infamous "color line" was Adrian "Cap" Anson, one of the greatest of the 19th century players. Anson was born in Marshalltown, Iowa, in 1852 and played baseball from 1871 to 1897, becoming the first player to reach the 3000-hit plateau. Though Anson died in 1922 (and made the Hall of fame in 1939), in one unfortunate respect he continued to influence the game of baseball for the next quarter-century.

The crucial incident took place in 1884, when Anson brought his Chicago White Stockings team to Newark, New Jersey, to play an exhibition game against some area minor leaguers. The Jersey team had a black pitcher named George Stovey, who once struck out 22 hitters in a game. When Anson heard that Stovey would be pitching against the White Stockings he said his team wouldn't take the field unless the pitcher was removed from the lineup. The New Jersey team complied, and after that Anson supposedly started a kind of crusade to keep blacks from playing alongside whites at any professional level.

Subsequently, a so-called "gentleman's agreement" in major league baseball cut off any attempts to put a black in uniform. Witness the case of Charlie Grant. He was an outstanding second baseman discovered by John McGraw when McGraw was managing the old Baltimore Orioles in 1901. But, with all his talents, Grant also happened to be black. Knowing that he couldn't slip Grant into the lineup as he was, McGraw tried to pass him off as a full-blooded Cherokee Indian. In the strangely warped world of racial prejudice an Indian was allowed to play ball but a black man was not.

McGraw's attempt at subterfuge failed when Charles Comiskey, the White Sox president, recognized Grant, whom he had seen play with the Chicago Columbia Eagles in the black leagues. From that point on, any black who may have played in the majors did so without the knowledge of baseball historians. The color line had been drawn.

As for the blacks, they formed their own leagues, called negro leagues then. The first pro-

**Above:** The Kansas City Monarchs were one of the great teams in the old negro leagues. Shown here with their team bus in 1936, the Monarchs had a number of players who would have made the majors had they not been black.

**Left:** Charles Comiskey, longtime owner of the Chicago White Sox, helped keep Charlie Grant out of the majors in 1901.

**Right:** Josh Gibson caught for the Homestead Grays from 1930 to 1946, more than once hitting 70 or more homers in a single season.

fessional all-negro team goes back as far as 1885. By 1920 the negro leagues had stabilized into a National negro league and a Negro Eastern League, and the two began their own World Series in 1924. Those leagues disbanded in 1932 during the Depression, but a few years later the Negro National and Negro American Leagues were formed and continued into the 1940s.

Some of the great black stars of those days are legendary now, and a number of them have been elected to the Hall of Fame. There is little doubt that the likes of Satchel Paige, Josh Gibson, Oscar Charleston, Judy Johnson, Cool Papa Bell, Leon Day, Ray Dandridge and others could not only have played in the major leagues of the 1920s and 1930s, but would certainly have been stars. Gibson, for instance, batted .457 in 1936 and .440 in 1938. He was a catcher who worked hard at improving all phases of his game.

Years later, when the color line had been broken and Roy Campanella was an all-star catcher for the Brooklyn Dodgers, someone asked him about Gibson, whom he had seen play

in the negro leagues. "I couldn't carry Josh's glove," Campy said. "Anything I could do, he could do better."

Satchel Paige, also, often played against major leaguers when the ballplayers barnstormed after the regular season. Though he finally reached the majors in 1948, Paige was then over 40 and obviously past his prime. But those who saw him pitch in the 1930s marveled at his skills. When Hack Wilson of the Cubs hit 56 homers and drove home a record 190 runs in 1930 he faced Paige in an exhibition game after the season ended. Wilson, like many others, couldn't touch Paige. "It looked like he was winding up with a baseball and throwing a pea," Wilson said. In another exhibition game in 1934 Paige faced Dizzy Dean of the Cardinals, who had won 30 games that year. The two righthanders matched serves for 13 innings. When it ended, Dean had struck out 15 and had given up just one run. But Paige had fanned 17 and tossed a shutout!

Several teams had made overtures to black players during the desperation of the war years,

JACK ROOSEVELT ROBINSON

BROOKLYN N.L. 1947 TO 1956
LEADING N.L. BATTER IN 1949. HOLDS
FIELDING MARK FOR SECOND BASEMAN
PLAYING IN 150 OR MORE GAMES WITH .992.
LEAD N.L. IN STOLEN BASES IN 1947 AND
1949. MOST VALUABLE PLAYER IN 1949.
LIFETIME BATTING AVERAGE .311. JOINT
RECORD HOLDER FOR MOST DOUBLE PLAYS
BY SECOND BASEMAN, 137 IN 1951.
LED SECOND BASEMEN IN DOUBLE
PLAYS 1949-50-51-52.

**Above:** Leroy "Satchel" Paige was one of the great pitchers of all time. Yet he was forced to toil for a year in the negro leagues before coming to the majors as a 41-year-old rookie in 1948.

**Above right:** This plaque honoring Jackie Robinson at Cooperstown is testament to both his ability as a ballplayer and his courage as a man.

but this only led to a few aborted tryouts. Thus, during April of 1945 Jackie Robinson, Sam Jethroe and another black were called to Boston for an alleged tryout with the Red Sox. They went through the motions and were sent home with a don't-call-us-we'll-call-you goodbye. One story had it that the Red Sox conducted the tryout only because they were seeking favorable Sunday baseball legislation in Massachusetts.

But when Branch Rickey told his scouts to look at some of the best black baseball talent in America, he was serious. He did it under the guise of starting yet another negro league. But he knew exactly what he wanted and why he wanted it. Indeed, Rickey had made a casual remark as early as 1943 to George McLaughlin, president of the Brooklyn Trust Company, the bank that guided the team's board of directors. Rickey was then talking about signing 15- and 16-year-olds in anticipation of the war's end in another year or two. "We're going to beat the bushes, and we'll take whatever comes out," the man known as the Mahatma told McLaughlin, "and that might include a negro player or two."

When McLaughlin didn't object, Rickey put his plan into action. After screening a number of the best black ballplayers in the country, he felt he had found his man: Jack Roosevelt Robinson. The two men met in late August 1945 in what proved to be a historic confrontation.

Rickey revealed his plan to Robinson and then preceeded to tell the 26-year-old former four-letter star from UCLA just how difficult it would be to implement. He knew Robinson was intelligent and well-educated. He also knew that Jackie was a man who spoke out when he saw things that weren't right. In fact, Robinson had gone through an army court martial because he refused to step to the back of a bus traveling on an army post. Robinson had won, and the charges were dropped.

He also knew that Robby was an outstanding athlete. He was one of the finest running backs ever to play for the UCLA football team, was an excellent basketball player, a track star, as well as a baseball performer with fine all-around skills. He had played for the Kansas City Monarchs in the negro leagues but, despite being one of the team's stars, he had left because of the lackluster way the league and many of the games were run. He was also disappointed by thc sham of the tryout in Boston that April. But it didn't take Jackie Robinson long to realize that the 63-year-old man sitting across the table from him was dead serious.

In describing some of the things he thought would happen, Rickey used every racial epithet

he could think of, creating scenerios that caused Robinson to break out in a sweat. Then he told Robinson that he would have to take the insults and maybe even the physical abuse.

"Mr Rickey," asked the puzzled Robinson, "do you want a ballplayer who's afraid to fight back?"

Without pausing, Rickey answered, "I want a ballplayer with guts enough *not* to fight back. You'll have to do this thing with base-hits, stolen bases and by fielding ground balls. Nothing else!"

Rickey persuaded Robinson that he would have to turn the other cheek for at least the first year. Obviously, Rickey didn't want to give anyone an excuse to suspend Robinson or throw him out of the league. And he knew that some people would try. When he was convinced that Jackie Robinson was the right man for the job, he signed him to an historic contract. Baseball was about to be revolutionized, but not right away. It was decided that Robinson would spend the 1946 season at the Dodgers' top farm team in Montreal. He would come up to the Bigs in 1947.

It wasn't easy for Robinson or Rickey that first year. Montreal trained in Florida with the Dodgers, and Robinson was treated cruelly by both fans and opposing players – even by some of his new teammates. The president of the minor leagues called Rickey a "carpetbagger" and cracked that there would be a Rickey Temple constructed in Harlem. But Robinson did do what Rickey had told him to do, answer his critics with basehits, and he led the International League in hitting, with a .349 average.

When the 1946 season began not too many people in the big leagues were thinking about Jackie Robinson. Rather, it was first things first, and there was the business of getting the majors back to normal as well as hoping that all the returning stars could regain their former skills despite losing up to four years to military service. But before even those questions could be answered there was still another problem. A new baseball league was trying to steal players from the majors.

Called the Mexican League, it was begun by a wealthy Mexican named Jorge Pasquel who, along with his millionaire brothers, felt it was time for a new league south of the border. The Pasquels promised better salaries, newer ballparks and competitive pennant races. Mexico had had professional baseball since 1925, but this was the first time they had made a pitch for American players.

The move wasn't without precedent. Back in 1913 an attempt was made to convert the Federal League from a minor league into a major league, and the men running it began raiding the majors for talent. Several well-known players actually jumped to the Federal League, while others used it as a lever to gain higher salaries from their teams. The Federal League lasted for two seasons (1914 and 1915) before folding, but it did give rise to a number of new ballparks, including Wrigley Field in Chicago, which is still in use today.

So when the Mexican League was born in 1945 baseball people took it seriously. Commissioner Chandler declared it an "outlaw" league and said that any players jumping south of the border would be barred from returning to the majors for five years. Yet a number of players went, most of them from the National League.

**Opposite above:** Jackie Robinson slides to second while playing for Montreal in 1946.

**Opposite left:** At Montreal Robby showed he was ready for the big leagues.

**Above right:** Sal "The Barber" Maglie was one of the top players to jump to the Mexican League in 1945.

**Right:** Stan Musial rejected a Mexican offer and stayed with the Cards.

**Opposite:** Leo Durocher (l) and Branch Rickey when they were running the Dodgers in 1943.

**Above:** The Cards and Red Sox prepare to square off in the 1946 World Series before a packed house at old Sportsman's park in St Louis.

The Giants, for instance, lost seven players, including pitcher Sal Maglie and relief star Ace Adams. The Cards lost Max Lanier, one of their top pitchers, as well as two other players. Catcher Mickey Owen, who had dropped the famous third strike in the 1941 World Series, defected from the Dodgers. But no so-called superstars jumped. In fact, the Mexicans offered Stan Musial a $65,000 advance and a five-year package worth some $130,000 per year, but the Man decided to remain with the Cardinals.

It didn't take long for the jumpers to find that baseball life in Mexico wasn't ideal. The weather was extremely hot and so was the food. Bad water often made the players' sick. Those who had gone south were quickly disenchanted, and most returned within two years.

The question was how to deal with them. Mickey Owen, for instance, returned to the States as early as August 1946. Could Commissioner Chandler really keep him out of baseball for five more years? Another returning jumper, Danny Gardella of the Giants, actually took the matter to court. As it turned out, most of those who returned from Mexico were back in the majors within two or three years at the most.

There was another event in the spring of 1946 that would have far-reaching affects on the future of the game. A Harvard Lawyer named Robert Murphy formed the American Baseball Guild to represent the players against the owners. Many players were unhappy with their salaries, and a strike atmosphere that permeated the entire country was close to spreading to baseball.

It was rumored in June that the Pittsburgh Pirates were close to striking against their owner, Bill Benswanger. The baseball brass did not want the formation of a players' union, so they asked for delegates to discuss the situation. And by September 1946 the owners made their first concessions to the players as a group. They included a $5000 minimum salary, a limit of salary cuts to 25 percent per year and a pension fund which would grow through club payments. Other new benefits included a shorter spring training period, free medical coverage and a $25-per-week cash allowance during spring training.

Because of the concessions made by Commissioner Chandler and the owners the players in 1946 didn't form a permanent union, but their actions and the resultant concessions from management would lead some years later to the formation of the Major League Baseball Players'

Association, a strong union that helped make the ballplayer among the best paid employees in the land, with a superb pension and benefit package. The seeds of that were sown in 1946.

The lords of the game were right about one thing. With the war over and the top players back, attendance jumped. The National League would go from a low of 3,769,342 fans in 1943 to a record-breaking 8,902,107 in 1946. The American League also set a new mark of 9,621,182, a far cry from the 3,696,569 who passed through the turnstyles three years earlier.

And the product was once again first class. In the National League the Cardinals and Dodgers resumed their battle for the top spot. Stan Musial, who had missed only one year, seemed better than ever, and he had fine support from Cardinal teammates such as Enos Slaughter, Red Schoendienst, Terry Moore, Marty Marion, Whitey Kurowski and pitchers Harry Breecheen, Howie Pollet and Murray Dickson. Musial would wind up leading the league in hitting, with a .365 average, and also top the senior circuit in doubles, triples, hits, slugging percentage, total bases and runs scored.

The Dodgers would soon be a team in transition, but they hung in there with the likes of veterans Dixic Walker, Cookie Lavagetto, Pee Wee Reese and Eddie Stanky. They also had youngsters like Carl Furillo and Bruce Edwards, as well as some seasoned pitchers in Hugh Casey, Hal Gregg and Ralph Branca. Spurred on by their fiery manager, Leo Durocher, the Dodgers hung tough, and the two teams finished in a dead tie, forcing the first pennant playoff in history. But the Cardinals' superior firepower finally prevailed, and St Louis won it by taking two straight playoff games.

In the American League the big stars were also making noise. Hank Greenberg belted 44 home runs and drove in 127 runs to lead the league in both departments. Washington's Mickey Vernon took the batting title, with a .353 mark. Joe DiMaggio, however, had someting of an off year, with 25 homers, 95 RBIs and a .290 batting mark. A painful bone spur on his heel slowed DiMag and helped slow the Yankees as well.

In Cleveland, Bob Feller returned with a bang from nearly four years of military service. Still only 27 years old, Rapid Robert won 26 games while losing 15. He led the league, with 371 innings pitched, and set a modern major league record of 348 strikeouts. Some baseball historians would later say that a re-checking of the records showed that Rube Waddell had fanned 349 in 1904, but Feller's achievement was awesome nevertheless.

Then there were the Red Sox. Led by Ted Williams, the Bosox put it all together, winning

104 games and their first American League pennant since 1918, 12 games over the Detroit Tigers. As he would later do after the Korean conflict, the Splendid Splinter returned to the game without missing a beat. Playing in 150 games, Ted hit .342, swatted 38 homers and drove home 123 runs. He didn't lead the league

**Left:** Cleveland's Bob Feller in action in 1946, the year he struck out 348 hitters.

**Below:** Back from the war in 1946, Ted Williams was still a great hitter. Here, the Splinter gets congrats from team-mate Bobby Doerr after hitting a homer.

**Opposite right:** DiMaggio hits foul off a Bob Feller fastball in 1946. Both Rapid Robert and the Yankee Clipper are in the Baseball Hall of Fame.

in any of those categories, but he put it all together better than anyone else and was named the league's Most Valuable Player for the season.

Ted didn't do it alone. Centerfielder Dom DiMaggio, Joe's little brother and a fine player in his own right, batted .316 for the year. Shortstop Johnny Pesky hit .335, while Bobby Doerr and Rudy York also made major contributions at the plate. Righthander Dave Ferriss won 25 games, and Tex Hughson 20. Lefty Mickey Harris had his best year ever at 17-9, giving the Bosox a big three on the hill. Going into the World Series, most experts rated it a tossup.

To some it would be a battle of MVPs, Musial and Williams, but as is usually the case in the Series, the supporting players sometimes upstage the stars. St Louis took a 2-1 lead into the ninth inning of the first game at Sportsman's Park with Howie Pollet on the mound. But Boston tied it when Pinky Higgins got a bad-hop basehit to drive in a run. And it ended in the tenth when Rudy York belted a home run off Pollet to give the Bosox a 1-0 lead.

Game two was all Harry Brecheen. The crafty Cardinal lefthander, known as the "Cat," threw a four-hit shutout at the Red Sox as the Cards defeated Mickey Harris 3-0 to even the Series at a game apiece. With the Series shifting back to

**Opposite top:** Dom DiMaggio of the Red Sox is tagged out at home by the Cards' Joe Garagiola during 1946 World Series action.

**Above:** One of the best outfielders in the game, Dom DiMaggio makes a leaping grab at Boston's Fenway Park.

**Opposite left:** Harry "The Cat" Brecheen of the Cards beat the Red Sox three times during the 1946 World Series, compiling a trifling 0.45 ERA.

Boston for game three the Red Sox had their turn, Dave Ferriss throwing a six-hit shutout and winning 4-0. Rudy York was the batting star, with two hits, including a homer and three RBIs. The Bosox had a 2-1 lead in games, and neither Musial nor Williams had yet been a factor at the plate.

The fourth game quickly turned into a rout. The Cards erupted for 20 hits off Tex Hughson and relievers, winning an easy 12-3 victory behind George Munger. Three runs in the second and three more in the third gave the Cards a big early lead. Slaughter, Kurowski and catcher Joe Garagiola had four hits apiece for the Cards, while Marty Marion had three. The easy win evened the Series once more, this time at two games each.

In game five the seesaw pattern continued. Joe Dobson tossed a four-hitter for the Red Sox, as the Beantowners took a 6-3 win to go ahead once again. Now the Sox just had to win one of two games in St Louis to nail down the championship. And they sent Mickey Harris to the mound once again to face the wily Harry Brecheen.

The Cards parlayed a succession of basehits into three runs in the third inning, and Brecheen made them stand up. He kept the Red Sox off balance with a variety of curves and off speed pitches and went the distance for the second time in the Series, taking a 4-1 decison that evened things at three games each. So the baseball world watched as the two teams battled into a seventh and deciding game. And it was quickly noted that the Cards had never lost a World Series that went the distance, having won in 1926, 1931 and 1934. The Red Sox hoped to put an end to that streak.

Seventh-game pitchers were Murray Dickson for the Cardinals and Dave Ferriss for the Bosox. The Sox got on the board with a run in the first, but St Louis promptly tied it with a tally in the second. It stayed that way until the fifth, when the Cards KOed Ferriss and pushed a pair of runs across, giving them a 3-1 lead. Meanwhile, Dickson was sailing along, keeping the Red Sox batters at bay. When the Sox came up in the eighth they had just six outs left.

But to the Bosox' credit, they didn't quit. Manager Joe Cronin called on a pair of pinch hitters to open the frame, and both delivered. Glen Russell started it with a single to center. Then, with the tension building, George Metkovich doubled him to third. Cardinal Manager Eddie Dyer then replaced Dickson with his most effective pitcher, Harry Brecheen, who had gone a full nine innings just two days earlier. When Bre-

**Above:** Enos Slaughter slides across home plate with the run that won the 1946 Series for the Cards. Slaughter scored from first on a double by Harry Walker.

cheen struck out Wally Moses, then induced Johnny Pesky to hit a liner to short right, Enos Slaughter's throw holding the runners, it looked as if he would pitch the Cards out of the jam.

Now, with two out, he was facing Dom DiMaggio. The Little Professor waited for his pitch and then slammed a clutch double, driving in Russell and Metkovich. The game was tied at 3-3. Brecheen got the next hitter, but the damage was done. Could the Cardinals now regain the momentum?

Bob Klinger was on the hill for the Sox as the Cards came to bat. Enos Slaughter led off with a single, but Klinger toughened and retired both Whitey Kurowsky and Del Rice, bringing Harry "The Hat" Walker to the plate. Walker smacked a basehit to left center, and Slaughter took off. He steamed past second as Red Sox centerfielder Leon Culberson picked the ball up and threw it to shortstop Pesky, who had run out to take the relay.

Pesky must have figured Slaughter would stop at third, for he hesitated a second, only to see the Cardinal outfielder steaming toward home. His throw arrived a hair too late, and Slaughter slid across the plate with the go-ahead run. "Slaughter's Mad Dash," as it's often called, proved to be the winning run, for Brecheen retired the Red Sox in the ninth, winning his third victory of the Series.

For years people talked about Slaughter scoring all the way from first on a single. Actually, Walker was credited with a double on the hit, but the play was still one of the most dramatic in World Series history, and it made the Cardinals world champions once more. Walker led the Cardinal hitters, with a .412 average and six RBIs, while the heroic Slaughter batted .320 in the seven games. For the Red Sox, Bobby Doerr batted .409, while Rudy York supplied the power with two homers and five ribbys.

And what about the battle of the MVPs, Musial and Williams? Surprisingly, neither was a factor. Stan the Man hit only .222, with six hits and four RBIs. The Splendid Splinter did even more of a disappearing act. He had just five singles in 25 at bats, for a .200 average and one run batted in, proving once again that you never know in baseball. But it was an exciting Series and a fitting end to a most interesting baseball

season. But it pales in comparison to what was about to happen in 1947.

A preview of the next year came toward the end of the 1946 when one sports columnist began reviewing baseball's first postwar season, mentioning that players like Ted Williams, Bob Feller, Dixie Walker and Hal Newhouser were all having great seasons. But then the columnist added, "The greatest performance being put on anywhere in sport . . . is being supplied by . . . Jackie Robinson of Montreal, who is playing baseball under pressures that would have crushed a less courageous man."

When spring training opened, Jackie Robinson was still officially on the roster of the Montreal team. Rickey didn't want to stir people up before he had to. But he had already signed two more blacks – pitcher Don Newcombe and catcher Roy Campanella – to Montreal contracts. So now nearly everyone guessed that the Mahatma was about to break the color line in Brooklyn.

There was a diversion, however, as spring training moved into its final stages. Dodger manager Leo Durocher had been feuding with one of his former bosses who was now running another ballclub. Leo the Lip began going to the press, making the feud public. He told the press that his old boss had been entertaining two known gamblers at a ballgame, and since he had already been admonished for his own propensity for placing a bet, he questioned whether there was a double standard for owners and managers.

The sniping continued until Commissioner Chandler felt it was time to take action. He decided to suspend the controversial manager for one year, the reason cited being Durocher's "conduct detrimental to baseball." The suspension was considered harsh, but it held neverthe-

less. Some thought the severity of the penalty came, in part, from Chandler's personal dislike for Durocher. But the action forced Branch Rickey to find another skipper for the Dodgers, and he turned to veteran Burt Shotton.

Then, with about a week remaining before the opening of the season, and just two days after Durocher's suspension, Rickey announced that the Dodgers had purchased the contract of Jackie Robinson from Montreal. Major league baseball would at last have a black man as part of its opening day roster. Since Eddie Stanky was the Dodgers' second baseman, it was decided that Robinson would open the season at first. And when the Dodgers took the field against the Boston Braves for their first game of 1947, baseball's color line finally fell.

Jackie went hitless that day against Boston's crafty Johnny Sain. "All I saw from Sain was curve balls," Robinson recalled, "curves of different sizes, shapes and speeds, and I wondered if maybe I'd soon be back in Montreal."

**Above left:** Jubilant Cards carry Harry Brecheen off the field after his third win over the Red Sox.

**Above right:** Bobby Doerr was a top Red Sox second sacker for 15 years.

**Below:** Jackie Robinson and Branch Rickey shake hands to cement their agreement that would make Robby the first black player in the major leagues.

But Rickey and everyone who had seen him knew that Jackie Robinson could play. His first hit was a bunt single the very next day, and in his third game he belted his first major league home run off Dave Koslo of the New York Giants. He was on his way. He also began running into some of the things he had been warned about by Branch Rickey, but no matter what he heard from fans and opponents, Jackie remained true to his word and turned the other cheek.

The Philadelphia Phillies were one team that gave Robinson an especially difficult time. In one game the racial slurs became so harsh that his teammates sensed that Jackie might take off after some of the Phils. That's when Eddie Stanky suddenly hollared to Philly manager Ben Chap-

**Right:** On his first day in the big leagues Jackie Robinson was signing autographs for some young Brooklyn fans. However, it wouldn't always be this easy in 1947.

man, "Chapman, why don't you get on somebody who can fight back." At the same time, Pee Wee Reese, who was born in Kentucky, walked over and put his arm around Robinson's shoulder. It was a show of strength and support that would help Robinson get through his first season.

But life wasn't all roses for Robinson with the Dodgers, either. Several of the southern-born players began circulating a petition to get Jackie off the team. When Rickey found out about the move he said that anyone who didn't want to play with Jackie Robinson, or any other black man for that matter, would be traded. Southern-born Dixie Walker, so popular in Brooklyn that he was nicknamed the "Peepul's Cherce," did ask out, but he eventually finished the season in Brooklyn before moving on to Pittsburgh the following year.

Despite the constant pressure, Jackie Robinson began playing winning baseball. He wasn't a slugger by any means, but rather a slashing kind of hitter with home run power. And while he didn't have an overpowering throwing arm, he was an otherwise outstanding fielder who could make the big play. On the basepaths he was dazzling, a constant threat to steal who drove pitchers to distraction just by his very presence.

Although many still think of Jackie Robinson as the one and only black player of 1947, there were others coming into the Bigs before the year was out. At the end of August the Dodgers brought up a young black pitcher named Dan Bankhead, who appeared in six games by the end of the year. Bankhead was limited by talent rather than by the color of his skin.

And in the American League the Cleveland Indians brought up a big outfield slugger named Larry Doby, who would appear in 29 games during 1947 before becoming a regular the following year. Then, on 20 July, the St Louis Browns made a small bit of baseball history of their own when they became the first team to have two black players in the starting lineup at the same time. Playing against the Red Sox, the Browns started Williard Brown in right field and Hank Thompson at second base. Now young blacks could dream about playing baseball in the major leagues without having the dream turn into a nightmare.

While the big baseball news of 1947 was certainly the breaking of the color line, there were also a pair of pennant races and a spate of outstanding individual performances to fascinate fans in both leagues. In the National it was the Dodgers and Cardinals battling it out once again. The two teams had tied the year before, but with Jackie Robinson in the lineup the Dodgers had a little extra spark, and this time they won the pennant by five games.

**Top:** Ray Sanders, left, is welcomed to the Brooklyn Dodgers in 1948 by Pee Wee Reese and Jackie Robinson.

**Above:** Robinson was a line drive hitter with power, and a great competitor.

**Left:** Slugger Larry Doby of Cleveland was the first black to play in the American League, in 1947.

**Above:** Phil Rizzuto of the Yanks was a young rookie shortstop when this picture was taken in March, 1941.

**Below:** Catcher Yogi Berra joined the Yanks in 1946 and became a big part of the Bomber dynasty.

The American League race wasn't even that close. After a mediocre third-place finish in 1946 the Yankees came roaring back. They broke it open with a 19-game winning streak in July and finished a very comfortable 12 games ahead of the Detroit Tigers. Like the Dodgers, the Yankees were a team in transition. They still had great veterans such as DiMaggio and Tommy Henrich, a tremendous shortstop in Phil Rizzuto and some adequate role players like Johnny Lindell, George McQuinn and Snuffy Stirnweiss. But they also had a fine young catcher in Yogi Berra, a pair of hard-throwing righthanders named Allie Reynolds and Vic Raschi and a reliever par excellence in Joe Page.

For the Dodgers, Robinson had joined Stanky and Reese in the infield. Dixie Walker, Carl Furillo and the still-dangerous Pete Reiser patrolled the outfield. Bruce Edwards was the catcher, with Roy Campanella still a year away. The pitching staff featured 21-game winner Ralph Branca and reliever Hugh Casey. Otherwise, their pitching was spotty. As usual, the Yanks were heavy favorites to win the World Series.

Before the Series began baseball had a chance to look back at its second postwar season. Robinson was the biggest story of the year, and despite living in a fishbowl and enduring the worst kind of racial taunting, he had produced a fine season. Playing in 151 games Robby hit a solid .297, with 12 homers and 48 RBIs. He had 175 hits, 31 doubles and five triples, and he swiped 29 bases. For his efforts he became baseball's first-ever Rookie of the Year.

But Jackie wasn't the only player making noises in the National League in 1947. A second-year slugger for the Pittsburgh Pirates, Ralph Kiner, clubbed 51 home runs. He had led the league as a rookie, with 23, the year before and would win or tie for the home run title in the senior circuit for seven straight seasons.

The 1947 season was one of those in which he tied, for big John Mize of the Giants also belted 51 and was part of a team that set a record of 221 round-trippers for the season. Though they finished in fourth place, the Giants had a slugging team that year. Besides Mize's contribution, Willard Marshall hit 36, Walker Cooper smacked 35 and Bobby Thomson cracked 29.

There were also five 20-game winners in the senior circuit that year. Joining the Dodgers' Branca were Warren Spahn and Johnny Sain of the Braves, along with Larry Jansen of the Giants and Ewell Blackwell of the Cincinnati Reds. Blackwell finished the year with a 22-8 mark, including 16 victories in succession.

Blackwell was something of a curiosity. A very tall, very thin righthander who buggy-whipped the ball sidearm to hitters, he put together his finest season in 1947. In fact, Blackwell never won 20 games again and finished his career with a mediocre, 82-78 record. Yet many of the righthanded hitters of his day called "The Whip" the toughest pitcher they ever faced.

But in 1947 he was virtually unbeatable. In mid-June Blackwell came close to tying one of baseball's seemingly untouchable records, that

of pitching two no-hitters in a row. It had been done in 1938 by Johnny VanderMeer of Cincinnati, still a teammate of Blackwell's in 1947. On 18 June The Whip threw a no-hitter against the Braves, and four days later faced the Dodgers. Once again he began working his sidearm magic, and the Dodger hitters couldn't touch him. He was just two outs away in the ninth inning when Eddie Stanky slapped a single right through his legs and up the middle. On the bench, someone

**Far left:** Slugger Ralph Kiner of Pittsburgh tied or led the National League in homers for seven years in a row.

**Left:** Lefty Warren Spahn of the Braves won 20 or more games 13 times. Here the Hall of Fame hurler tunes up before the 1948 season.

**Below:** Big John Mize hit 359 homers during his career with the Cards, Giants and Yankees. Here the big guy shows his swing prior to the 1946 season.

asked VanderMeer what he would have done if his teammate had tied his record. "I would have been the first one out there to shake his hand," Vandy said.

In the American League it was more a hitter's year. Bob Feller was the only 20-game winner, with a 20-11 mark, but even Rapid Robert hadn't been as spectacular as he had the year before. Ted Williams made the most noise at the plate. The Splinter captured his second triple crown, with 32 home runs, 114 RBIs and a .343 batting average. Yet he wasn't named the league's Most Valuable Player.

That honor went to DiMaggio, even though Joe D's numbers weren't close to Williams'. The Yankee Clipper hit .315, with 20 homers and 97 runs batted in. The next year, however, 1948, DiMag would himself win two legs of the triple crown, with 39 homers and 155 RBIs, to go with a .320 batting average . . . and Lou Boudreau of Cleveland would be MVP. Baseball is sometimes a difficult game to explain.

But on to the World Series. As expected, whenever there was a Subway Series excitement in New York reached a fever pitch. And the teams – especially the Dodgers and Yanks – rarely let the fans down. They produced great moments.

The Series opened at Yankee Stadium with rookie Spec Shea going for the Yanks against Ralph Branca of the Dodgers. The Dodgers got a run in the first, and Branca retired the first 12 Bombers to face him. But in the fifth the Yanks reverted to type and scored five times to put the game away. Shea and reliever Joe Page did the rest, and the Bombers won it 5-3.

Game two was even easier. With 19-game winner Allie Reynolds on the hill, the Yanks coasted to a 10-3 victory, getting 15 hits off four Dodgers hurlers. They now had a 2-0 lead and looked as though they could do it with mirrors. Buy then the Series moved to cozy Ebbets Field in Brooklyn, and there the Dodgers felt at home.

Brooklyn erupted for six runs in the second inning of game three and had a 9-4 lead after four, hanging on for a 9-8 victory, their first win of the Series. Robinson, Furillo, Walker and John Jorgensen had two hits each for the winners. Then came game four, and this one nearly made baseball history of one kind, and then wound up in another way that will never be forgotten.

The Yanks started Floyd "Bill" Bevens, a journeyman righthander who had had just a 7-13 record in 1947. Yet on this October afternoon Bevens had perhaps the best stuff of his career. Except for the fact that he was somewhat wild, the Dodgers couldn't touch him. The Yanks got a run off Harry Taylor in the first and Hal Gregg

**Opposite top:** Righty Allie Reynolds won 182 games between 1942 and 1954, most with the Yanks.

**Opposite bottom:** 20-year-old Ralph Branca after tossing a three-hit shutout for the Dodgers in 1946.

**Above:** Brooklyn's Cookie Lavagetto pinch-hits the double that wins game 4 of the 1947 World Series.

in the fourth, while the Dodgers were getting nothing but an occasional walk off Bevens.

Then, in the fifth, the Dodgers got one back on a pair of walks, a sacrifice and an infield out. It was a 2-1 game, but Brooklyn still didn't have a basehit. And when the game reached the bottom of the ninth inning the same situation prevailed: the Yanks had a 2-1 lead, and the Dodgers still didn't have a single hit. Now the tension really mounted, for there had never been a no-hitter pitched in World Series history.

Once again Bevens went to work. He retired catcher Edwards for the first out but then walked Furillo, his eighth free pass of the game. After third baseman Jorgensen fouled out, Bevens was just a single out away from immortality. That's when Manager Shotton sent Al Gionfriddo in to run for Furillo. With Pete Reiser batting for pitcher Casey, Gionfriddo stole second base.

Yankee Manager Bucky Harris then decided to give Reiser an intentional pass. Because Pistol Pete had been hampered by a bad leg, fleet Eddie

Miksis went in to run for him. Now Eddie Stanky was due up, but Shotton called him back and sent veteran Cookie Lavagetto up to pitch hit. It was do or die for the Dodgers, as well as for Bill Bevens.

Cookie took the first pitch, then went after the second. He drove the ball down the rightfield line and off the wall. As Lavagetto chugged into second, both Gionfriddo and Miksis crossed home plate with the tying and winning runs. The Dodgers had not only won the game in dramatic fashion to tie the Series, but Cookie Lavagetto had broken up Bevens' bid for a no-hitter. It was one of the truly great finishes in the long history of the Fall Classic.

Game five was decided in the fifth inning when DiMaggio belted a homer off Rex Barney. Spec Shea threw a four-hitter as the Yanks won the game 2-1 and took a 3-2 lead in the Series. Now it was back to Yankee Stadium for the sixth encounter, Vic Lombardi of the Dodgers facing the Yanks' Allie Reynolds.

This one was another heartstopper. The Dodgers took a 4-0 lead by the top of the third, KOing Reynolds. But in the bottom of the frame the Bombers came back with four of their own to tie it. They got one more in fourth, for a 5-4 lead, but the Dodgers wouldn't quit. A four-run outburst in the top of the sixth enabled them to retake the lead at 8-5. Then came the bottom of the inning and another of baseball's memorable moments.

The Yanks had two on with two out when DiMaggio came to the plate. Facing Joe Hatten, the Yankee Clipper creamed one deep to left-center field. Al Gionfriddo, who had gone into the game as a defensive replacement in that very inning, raced back to the Yankee bullpen and made a sensational catch against the low fence, robbing DiMaggio of a potentially game-tying home run. From there the Dodgers went on to an 8-6 victory, knotting the Series at three-games each. So, as it so often does in Series play, it all

came down to a seventh and deciding game.

It was Spec Shea against Hal Gregg in the finale, and the Dodgers quickly got a pair in the top of the second, knocking out Shea and bringing Bevens into the game. The Yanks got one back in the second, then KOed Gregg in the fourth when pitch hitter Bobby Brown doubled home the tying run and Tommy Henrich singled home the go-ahead run. The Yanks then scored insurance tallies in the sixth and seventh, while Joe Page shut the Dodgers down on one hit over the final five innings. The game ended at 5-2, and the Yankees were once again World Champs.

While the World Series marked the beginning of some great careers – Robinson's, Berra's, Gil Hodges' – it also marked the end of others. Ironically, three of the central figures in the 1947 fall classic – Bill Bevens, Cookie Lavagetto, and Al Gionfriddo – were all released after the season and never played major league baseball again.

**Opposite:** The Dodgers' Cookie Lavagetto gets the royal treatment after his winning hit broke up Bill Bevens' no-hitter in the 1947 World Series.

**Below:** Al Gionfriddo made one of the great catches in World Series history with this grab of a Joe DiMaggio drive in 1947.

# CHAPTER IV
# ON TO A
# DYNASTY

Two of the best. Ted Williams (left) and Joe DiMaggio each had tremendous respect for each other's talents.

Most baseball people looked to the Yankees and Dodgers to repeat their pennant-winning ways as the 1948 season began. Little did anyone know then that neither team would make it to postseason play. But then no one could know that *after* 1948 there would not be a World Series without either the Yanks, Dodgers or Giants until 1967.

At the outset of 1948 no one was really thinking in terms of dynasties. The infusion of new talent made the futures of all teams difficult to predict. While black players didn't come into the majors in droves, they were obviously there to stay. And although the ugly face of prejudice would show itself in different places and in different situations for years to come, black players began making contributions to the game almost immediately.

The Dodgers, however, were a little dismayed when they saw Jackie Robinson report for spring training in 1948. Having been feted on the banquet circuit, Robby's weight had balooned from 190 to 230 pounds. During the off-season, Brooklyn had traded Eddie Stanky so that Robinson could take over at second. But now Jackie had to lose a great deal of weight, and that undoubtedly contributed to his slow start. He would never again come to camp out of shape.

With Robinson slowed and the pitching questionable, the Dodgers found themselves in a battle with the Boston Braves, the Cardinals and even the Pittsburgh Pirates. Leo Durocher was back from his suspension, but he wasn't getting along with Branch Rickey, who apparently liked to tinker with the lineup and would often suggest changes to the volatile skipper.

Then, in July, an announcement was made that shocked the baseball world. Horace Stoneham, the owner of the New York Giants, had asked Rickey for permission to talk with his former manager, Burt Shotton. Stoneham was looking for a replacement for Mel Ott, who had been a great player with the Giants but was less successful as a manager. Stoneham's inquiry was met by a surprising reply. Rickey told the Giants owner that Shotton wasn't available . . . but that Leo Durocher was!

On 16 July the deal was finalized, with Durocher's approval, of course. Leo the Lip became manager of the rival Giants, while Shotton was recalled to run the Dodgers. Ott wasn't axed, for he was given a position in the Giants' front office.

As for the pennant race, it remained close, but the Braves' pitching was beginning to tell the story. Righthander Johnny Sain was en route to a 24-win season, while lefty Warren Spahn, who would someday become the winningest lefthander in baseball history, would follow up a 21-win 1947 season with 15 more in 1948. The Braves began to rely so much on their one-two punch that the team slogan became: "Spahn and Sain, then pray for rain."

When the smoke cleared the Braves had pulled away to win the pennant by six and a half games over the Cardinals, with the Dodgers another game back and the Pirates a game behind them.

The Cards might not have been that close had it not been for Stan Musial. Stan the Man simply put together the greatest season of his career. He won the National League batting title with a career-high .376 average. He also led the league in hits, with 230, runs scored, with 135, doubles, with 46, triples, with 18, and runs batted in, with

**Below:** Dodger manager Leo Durocher has a chat with Rookie of the Year Jackie Robinson in December, 1947.

**Left:** By 1949 Jackie Robinson was a bona fide star in the National League. In February Robby signed a new Dodger pact under the watchful eye of Branch Rickey (r) and Manager Burt Shotton.

**Below:** Seven-time National League batting champ Stan Musial was a record-setting star for the Cards from 1941 to 1963. The Man finished with 3630 hits and a .331 lifetime average.

131. He missed the triple crown because he hit "only" 39 home runs, one short of co-leaders Ralph Kiner and John Mize. As expected, the Man was the National League MVP by a wide margin.

Jackie Robinson also had another good year, hitting .296, with 12 homers and 85 RBIs, and that after a slow start. The Rookie of the Year in the senior circuit was shortstop Alvin Dark of the Boston Braves, who batted .322.

Over in the American League it was also pitching that ultimately made the difference in the pennant chase. Three teams were locked in a season-long struggle for the AL crown. The Yankees, with DiMaggio, the Red Sox, with Williams and the Cleveland Indians, with pitching. But that's really an over-simplification, because all three teams were very solid, top to bottom.

Still, there was no denying that the Indians had the arms. Bob Feller, at age 29, showed some signs of slowing down, with a rather mediocre 19-15 record. But righthander Bob Lemon and lefty Gene Bearden would both win 20. And in midseason the Indians made an acquisition that many thought was simply a publicity move, but one that turned out to be quite beneficial for the ballclub.

The team signed pitcher Leroy "Satchel" Paige, the legendary righthander who had dazzled fans in the negro leagues for so many years. Old Satch had just turned 42 (some think he was even older) when he joined the Tribe, and he was obviously well past his prime. But the old

man still knew how to pitch, and he made 21 appearances for the Indians down the stretch, compiling a 6-1 record and 2.47 earned run average. The pity of it was that most baseball fans never had the chance to see Paige in his prime, for he had compared favorably with the best of them.

The three clubs stayed close all the way, as each had a big hitter leading the way. For the Yanks Joe DiMaggio put together a super season, leading the league in both homers (38) and RBIs (155), while hitting .320. For Boston Ted Williams was up to his usual tricks, taking the batting title with a .369 mark and adding 25 home runs and 127 RBIs to his credits. And in Cleveland there was Lou Boudreau.

Boudreau was not only the team's shortstop, but its manager as well. He had first become playing manager in 1942 at the age of 24. Known as the Boy Wonder then, he still held the job in 1948 and produced the best offensive season of his career, batting .355 and authoring a brace of clutch hits. But the performance that allowed him to capture the MVP award over the likes of Williams and DiMaggio may have come on the last day of the season.

It was actually an extra day, because when the season ended the American League had its first-ever tie. Both Boston and Cleveland finished with identical 96-58 records. Unlike the National League, which had had a best of three playoff to break its tie in 1946, the American League scheduled a one-game playoff to decide its champion.

The game was played at Boston's Fenway Park, where it was thought the Sox and Williams would have the advantage. But it was Boudreau and Bearden who stole the show. The Cleveland manager turned all player as he slammed a pair of homers and two singles to lead the Tribe offense, while Bearden stymied the Bosox bats. The Indians won 8-3, giving them their first pennant since 1920.

It was a battle of aces at Braves Field in Boston when Bob Feller took the mound against Johnny Sain. Feller had been waiting for ten years for a chance to win a World Series game and he didn't want to blow it. Rapid Robert was brilliant, but so was the curveballing Sain. The two hurlers matched goose-eggs for seven innings, and it began to look as if the first break would win the ballgame. Sain retired the Tribe in the top of the eighth, and Feller went out to face the Braves once more.

When leadoff hitter Bill Salkeld drew a walk, Phil Masi went in to run for him. Mike McCormick sacrificed Masi to second, and Boudreau ordered Eddie Stanky walked intentionally. Then came a key play. Feller suddenly whirled

**Left:** Lefthander Gene Bearden was outstanding for Cleveland in the World Series of 1948.

**Bottom left:** Shortstop Lou Boudreau, AL MVP in 1948, also managed the Indians.

**Opposite above:** Alvin Dark, top shortstop for four N L teams, 1946-1960.

**Below:** The Braves' Johnny Sain, after shutting out the Indians in the '48 Series opener.

and fired the ball to shortstop Boudreau, who had cut in behind Masi at second. Umpire Bill Stewart called Masi safe, sending Boudreau into a rage, for the shortstop was certain the pickoff had worked.

But when Sain flied out it looked as if the argument might be academic. Tommy Holmes was up next. Always a fine contact hitter, Holmes smacked a single, sending Masi across the plate with what proved to be the winning run. Sain retired the Tribe in the ninth to complete a four-hit shutout. Bob Feller had given up just two hits en route to a heartbreaking 1-0 World Series defeat.

Cleveland wasn't about to roll over, however, not with the depth of their pitching staff. They quickly showed it in game two when Bob Lemon took to the mound and easily bested Warren Spahn 4-1. And this time the Braves couldn't pray for rain. With the Series moving back to Cleveland, Gene Bearden tossed a five-hit shut-

**Above:** A packed house in Cleveland celebrates as the Indians' Larry Doby crosses home plate after homering off Johnny Sain in game four of the '48 Series.

**Left:** Brave Earl Torgeson is put out by Lou Boudreau during game 2 of the 1948 Series on a pickoff throw from pitcher Bob Lemon.

**Opposite top:** Warren Spahn teamed with righty Johnny Sain to give the Braves a great one-two mound punch in 1948.

**Opposite bottom:** Dale Mitchell scores another Cleveland run during the 1948 World Series.

out and won 2-0, giving the Tribe a 2-1 edge.

Then, in the fourth game, the Indians had the luxury of pitting nine-game winner Steve Gromek against Sain. Perhaps it was a gamble on the part of Boudreau, but it paid off. Gromek won the game 2-1, giving up seven hits. Sain yielded just five hits, but single runs in the first and third innings did him in and gave the Tribe a comfortable 3-1 lead in games. One of the Indian runs was the result of a big Larry Doby home run, the first ever hit by a black man in Series history.

The next afternoon, Sunday, 10 October, a record-breaking crowd of 86,288 fans jammed huge Municipal Stadium to watch Bob Feller try to wrap up the Series against surprise starter Nelson Potter. Everyone figured that Feller would finally win his long-time-coming World Series game. But that round baseball can some-times take some mighty strange bounces.

Boston jumped on Rapid Robert for three runs in the first inning and another in the third, Bob Elliott hitting a pair of home runs. The fire-baller obviously didn't have his best stuff. But when the Indians bounced back with a run in the first and four more in the fourth to take a 5-4 lead, the huge Cleveland crowd began hoping their hero would settle down and hang on for the victory. But then Boston tied it in the fifth, and it was again anyone's game.

Feller was still in there, only now he was facing

Warren Spahn, who had replaced Potter in the fourth. Then, in the Boston sixth, the veteran righthander lost it completely. The Braves scored six times in the inning, driving Feller from the mound and ultimately to another World Series defeat. The final score was 11-5, and the Bostonians had pulled to 3-2 in games. One quick postscript on this one. Satchel Paige pitched two-thirds of an inning in the contest, giving the aging veteran a chance to appear in a World Series and making him the first black pitcher to do so. It should have happened a lot sooner.

Now it was back to Boston for the sixth game. The Indians had Bob Lemon primed and ready, while the Braves were forced to go with Bill Voi-selle, a 13-game winner during the regular sea-son. Cleveland took a 1-0 lead in the third, only to have the Braves tie it an inning later. But when the Tribe got a pair in the sixth and one more in the top of the eighth off reliever Spahn, they had a 4-1 lead and were just six outs away from the championship.

The Braves made a last-ditch effort in their half of the eighth inning. They loaded the bases with just one out, and manager Boudreau re-placed starter Lemon with Gene Bearden. The

**Left:** It's another happy scene as the Cleveland Indians leave the field after winning the 1948 Series from the Braves.

young lefty got Clint Conatser to fly out to left, but a run scored, making it 4-2. Then pinch hitter Phil Masi whacked a double, driving in the third Braves run. Suddenly, the game was on the line, with Mike McCormick up. McCormick hit a liner right back toward the mound. But Bearden managed to grab it for the third out. An inning later he retired the Braves once more, and the World Series was over.

There were a number of heroes. Bearden and Lemon pitched very well for the Tribe, while Larry Doby batted .318, with a homer. Earl Torgeson hit .380 and Bob Elliott .333 for the losing Braves. But the saddest story of the Series had to be Bob Feller. One of the greatest pitchers of his generation, Feller failed to win a game, losing twice, the first being the 1-0 heartbreaker. He must have wondered if he'd ever get another chance.

There was one other sad footnote to the 1948 season. The legendary Yankee great, Babe Ruth, died on 16 August, a victim of throat cancer. Baseball would miss the man who hit 60 home runs in 1927 and 714 for his career. He is often also credited with saving the game after the spectre of the Black Sox Scandal in 1919. The fans had returned to the game to see the mighty Bambino hit the ball a country mile out of ballparks all over the league. There would never be anyone else quite like him.

In 1949 Jackie Robinson reported to the Dodgers fit and trim and ready for a big year. It would be his third in the National League, and the furor over his signing had by now died down. But there still wasn't a stampede to sign black players, and some teams, for whatever reasons,

seemed downright reluctant to do so. The Dodgers would have Campanella and Newcombe with them in 1949, and both players would make immense contributions in years to come. The Giants also signed their first two blacks, Hank Thompson, who had played briefly with the St Louis Browns in 1947, and an outfielder from the Newark Eagles of the negro leagues, Monte Irvin.

Thompson would turn into little more than a journeyman player, but Irvin would have several outstanding seasons with the Giants and would ultimately win election to the Hall of Fame. He was 30 years old when he signed in 1949, still in

**Below:** Jackie Robinson and Roy Campanella flank Don Newcombe, who joined the Dodgers in May of 1949. Big Newk would be a three-time 20-game winner for the Brooks.

his prime, but not far from starting on the down-side. Most of his great years were spent in the negro leagues. In fact, Irvin would never forget the talent level of some of those teams. Re-marking on the 1946 Newark Eagles, he once said: "We had four really good pitchers. If we could have added another four or five, we could have put our club, intact, right into the major leagues. We were that good."

Irvin and Thompson wouldn't really contri-bute much to the Giants of 1949, both coming up in midseason after beginning the year in the minors. But Newcombe and Campanella would join Robinson to make a huge contribution to the Dodger effort that year and in years to come.

In the American League the big story would be not the arrival of a player, but the arrival of a manager. The junior circuit was much slower in signing blacks than the National League. Some have suggested that that was the reason the NL began dominating the All-Star Game in the 1950s and continued to do so into the 1960s. Just as an example, the New York Yankees, for all their greatness during the period, didn't have a black player until they brought up catcher Elston Howard in 1955. And the Red Sox, the last team to break its own color line, didn't sign black in-fielder Pumpsie Green until 1959.

But the Yanks did make a move in 1949 that would inevitably affect their immediate future and would provide baseball with the chance to enjoy one of its most beloved characters. The team had been hugely successful throughout the 1930s and early 1940s with Joe McCarthy at the helm. The longtime manager won a total of eight pennants and seven World Series with the Bombers. But McCarthy left after the 1946 sea-son and was replaced by Bucky Harris. Harris won in 1947, but when the club failed to repeat in 1948 he was dismissed.

The new manager was Charles Dillon Sten-gel, "Casey" to everyone, and a man who joined the Yanks without a very successful track record. Old Case had been a good ballplayer with several National League teams between 1912 and 1925. He had later managed the Dodgers and Boston Braves but had always been saddled with weak teams and, as a consequence, didn't produce a winner. He was 58 years old when the Yanks tabbed him and was managing in the Pacific

**Top left:** Casey Stengel became the new manager of the Yankees in 1949 and then won five consecutive pennants and World Series.

**Above:** Steady Eddie Lopat was part of a "Big Three" pitching staff that also included Vic Raschi and Allie Reynolds and helped the Yanks win glory.

Coast League, but it didn't take him long to make his mark in New York.

Stengel was first and foremost a baseball man. He had spent a lifetime in the game and had seen it grow and mature. He knew strategy and talent, and he had his own ideas about platooning players and setting up pitching rotations. And on top of all that he was an entertainer, a man who could tell baseball stories by the hour, spinning his yarns in a kind of weirdly mangled, malaprop language – soon dubbed "Stengelese" – that kept his listeners in stitches. Old Case was a character, all right, but he also turned out to be some manager.

Stengel also had the horses in 1949. Though the aging DiMaggio would only play in 76 games because of injury and illness, the Yanks had some other fine performers to pick up the slack. Berra was now an anchor behind the plate, just as Rizzuto was at shortstop. Old reliable Tommy Henrich had moved in to play first base. Young Jerry Coleman took over at second, while Bobby Brown and Billy Johnson split duties at third. Joining DiMag in the outfield were Gene Woodling, Hank Bauer, Cliff Mapes and Johnny Lindell. Veteran slugger Johnny Mize was a late-season pickup from the Giants and would help the team greatly over the next few years.

But it was the pitching that really made the difference in 1949. Stengel had a big three of right-handers in Vic Raschi, Allie Reynolds and crafty southpaw Eddie Lopat. In addition, Joe Page was still the fireman out of the bullpen, and those four formed the core of a fine staff. So rookie manager Stengel would have no excuse for not battling for the flag.

If anyone was going to challenge the Yanks in 1949 it would be the Red Sox. Boston had hitting to spare and a couple of fine pitchers. Besides the always-great Ted Williams the Sox could still count on the likes of Vern Stephens, Bobby Doerr, Dom DiMaggio and Johnny Pesky, while lefthander Mel Parnell and righty Ellis Kinder anchored the pitching staff.

In the National League the Dodgers were building a team similar to the Yanks, with outstanding players at nearly every position, most of them still young. Reese and Robinson were the keystone combo at short and second. Big Gil Hodges had taken over at first, and sure-handed Billy Cox moved in at third. Campanella was the National League's equal to Berra behind the plate. The outfield had power-hitting Duke Snider in center, strong-armed Carl Furillo in right and several players who alternated in left. Preacher Roe, Don Newcombe, Ralph Branca and Carl Erskine formed the nucleus of a fine pitching staff. This was essentially the team that would become known as the "Boys of Summer"

**Above:** Roy Campanella was a three-time MVP for the Dodgers and belted 242 home runs during his Dodger career.

and would challenge the Yanks for baseball supremacy for nearly a decade.

But despite the strength of both the Yanks and Dodgers, there were cliffhanger pennant races in both leagues in 1949. Boston and St Louis still had pennant potential and made it a race right down to the final day of the season.

The Yankee-Red Sox battle seesawed all year. The Indians, with their fine pitching, had hung tough for awhile but eventually dropped out of contention. That left it up to the old rivals to decide things. It was a year in which teammates Ted Williams and Vern Stephens would both drive home 159 runs to lead the league. And the Splinter would also crack a league-topping 43 homers to go with a .343 average. Those stats would earn him yet another Most Valuable Player award.

**Above:** The great Williams watches another one leave the park. Despite missing nearly five years to military service, the Splendid Splinter belted 521 career home runs.

After sitting out most of the first half with a painful bone spur on his heel DiMaggio got some key hits down the stretch, but then a case of pneumonia felled him near the end. Joe would bat .346, hit 14 homers and drive home 67 runs. Not bad for just 76 games.

Coming into the final two days of the season the Yanks still trailed the Red Sox by a game. As it happened, the two teams would be meeting head to head, so the Yanks could at least hold their fate in their own hands. Former Yankee skipper Joe McCarthy was piloting the Bosox, and that made the confrontation even more dramatic.

In the Saturday game DiMaggio made a surprise start, leaving his sickbed to inspire the team with a double and single. But the big blow was Johnny Lindell's home run in the eighth inning, enabling the Yanks to win 5-4 and tying the Sox for first. Joe Page got the win in relief of starter Reynolds.

On Sunday the Yanks did it again. Raschi was the pitcher, and young Jerry Coleman was the hero, with an eighth-inning, bases-loaded double that drove in three and sewed up a 5-3 victory. The Yanks had taken the pennant once again.

The National League race was between the Dodgers and Cards. It, too, was close, with the Dodgers finally prevailing by just a single game. Both the Dodgers and Yanks had won with identical 97-57 records, while the runners-up Cards and Red Sox both had 96-58 marks.

Jackie Robinson had really led the Dodgers in 1949, finally living up to the potential predicted for him. Free of Branch Rickey's initial restrictions to keep his mouth shut and turn the other cheek, Robby could now be more himself on the ballfield, and it showed in his performance. He led the league in hitting, with a .342 mark, smacked 16 homers, drove home 124 runs, swiped 37 bases and had 203 hits en route to winning the Most Valuable Player Award.

But Robby had plenty of help. Big Don Newcombe won the Rookie of the Year award (Washington slugger Roy Sievers won it in the AL) with a 17-8 record. Branca won 13, Roe 15 and young Carl Erskine ("Oisk" to many Brooklynites) came on strong with an 8-1 record. Campanella hit .287, with 22 homers and 82 RBIs, in his first full season. Snider hit .292, Hodges .285, Reese .279 and Carl Furillo banged away at a .324 clip. They were a hard-hitting, run-producing team.

So the city of New York buzzed with the excitement of another Subway Series. It would be the borough of the Bronx against the borough of Brooklyn. And the first two games, played at Yankee Stadium, produced a World Series first

Both Parnell, with 25, and Kinder, with 23, would crack the 20-victory mark. Bobby Doerr would hit .309, Dom DiMaggio .307 and John Pesky .306. Yet with all that firepower the Red Sox couldn't shake the Yanks. And many people gave much of the credit for that to the new manager, Casey Stengel.

All through the season the Yanks were beset by one injury after another. It was estimated that there were some 71 separate injuries to Yankee players that year, and Stengel had to platoon and manipulate his players constantly. He reached down to the far ends of his bench for names such as Dick Kryhoski, Jack Phillips and Fenton Mole, but he kept the club winning and right up there with the Red Sox. He still had his big three (Raschi won 21, Reynolds 17 and Lopat 15), and lefty Tommy Byrne became a dependable fourth starter with 15 victories. Even Page won 13 in relief, saving a bunch more.

**Top:** The three DiMaggio brothers, L to R, Joe, Vince and Dom, in 1946.

**Left:** An injured heel kept Joe D in civilian clothes early in the '49 season.

**Above:** Jackie Robinson shows the Most Valuable Player Award he won for the 1949 season, a year in which he led the N L with a .342 average and in which he drove home 124 runs.

**Above:** The Dodgers escort Preacher Roe from the field after the lanky lefthander shut out the Yanks on six hits in the second game of the 1949 World Series at Yankee Stadium.

**Right:** Bespectacled Jim Konstanty helped to bring relief pitching into the modern era with 16 wins and 22 saves in 74 games for the 1950 Phillies.

a pair of 1-0 shutouts. Allie Reynolds threw a two-hitter against the Dodgers in the first game, besting Don Newcombe. The lone tally came in the bottom on the ninth inning on a dramatic home run by Tommy Henrich. But the next day the tables were turned. Lefty Preacher Roe threw his variety of off-speed pitches at the Yanks and came away with a six-hit shutout and a win over Vic Raschi. The Dodgers got the only run in the second, when Robinson doubled and steamed home on a solid single by Hodges.

Then the Series moved to Ebbets Field in Brooklyn, where the noisy faithful flocked to see their beloved "Bums" in action. As it turned out, they didn't have much to cheer about. The Yanks turned on the magic and surprised everyone by winning three straight games by scores of 4-3, 6-4 and 10-6 to wrap up the championship in five games. Bobby Brown was the surprise hitting star for the Yanks, with a .500 average and five runs batted in. But neither team hit particularly well. The Yanks averaged just .226, and the Dodgers .210. The Bronx Bombers had the edge in pitching, and that was the difference. But both clubs were so strong that it was pretty obvious they would be meeting again in the upcoming seasons.

Repeating wouldn't be easy for the Yanks in 1950, but they would manage to do it. The Dodgers, however, would find that another fate awaited them. They would fall victim to an unlikely team of Philadelphia Phillies who will forever be known as the Whiz Kids.

Most baseball people figured the Dodgers would be challenged again by the Cardinals, and perhaps by the improving New York Giants under Leo Durocher. But the Phillies were improving too. As recently as 1945 the club was dead last, with a horrendous 46-108 record. That, of course, was a war year, but the team was generally thought of as a second-division ballclub, one that hadn't won a National League pennant in 35 years.

**Above:** Jackie Robinson trots home with Brooklyn's first run in the second game of the 1949 Series. Gil Hodges, whose single drove home Robinson, heads for first.

**Left:** Four heavy-hitting members of the 1950 Phils display their wares. Left to right, Willie Jones, Del Ennis, Andy Seminick and Dick Sisler.

During this time, however, owner Robert Carpenter had been rebuilding his team by stockpiling some fine young talent, and the ballclub was slowly getting better. In 1948 the Phils were still under .500, at 66-88. The following year they surprised many people by finishing third behind the Dodgers and Cards. But their 81-73 mark still left them some 16 games off the pace, so when 1950 began very few considered the Phillies bona fide contenders.

The team got out of the gate very quickly, and though most baseball people waited for them to fold, they didn't; the young players were holding up well. Not all of them are remembered now, but the club had Eddie Waitkus at first, fully recovered from a bullet wound sustained a year earlier when an obsessed woman fan had shot him in the chest. Mike Goliat was at second, Granny Hamner at short and Willie "Puddinhead" Jones at third. The outfield consisted of

big Del Ennis in left, fleet Richie Ashburn in center and, usually, Dick Sisler in right. Andy Seminick handled the catching, an important job, since it was the pitchers who took the Phils to the top.

Righthander Robin Roberts was the workhorse ace of the staff. In his third season with the Phils the 23-year-old righthander would become the team's first 20-game winner since 1917, with a 20-11 mark, and would go on to win 286 games in his career. He was backed up by 21-year-old Curt Simmons, who would go 17-8.

But perhaps the key to it all was a bespectacled 33-year-old righthander named Jim Konstanty. Konstanty had been little more than a journeyman since first coming up with Cincinnati in 1944. He had been with Boston briefly in 1946, then had gone back in the minors in 1947 before coming to the Phils in 1948 and appearing in just six games. The following year the Phils began using Konstanty out of the bullpen, and he

started finding himself, pitching in 53 games and posting a 9-5 record. Then, in 1950, he produced a super season. Making a then-record 74 appearances, Konstanty saved game after game, and when he wasn't doing that he was posting a 16-7 record. He was a pitcher manager Eddie Sawyer could turn to whenever there was trouble, and Konstanty almost always came through.

Despite some fine individual seasons by many of the Dodger stars, the Phils hung tough. They held the lead right into September, but then they were dealt a severe blow when Curt Simmons, who had already won 17 games, was inducted into the army. Without the young lefthander, the Philadelphia pitching was stretched thin, and even more of a burden fell on Robin Roberts. With just 11 games left, the Phils had a seemingly safe lead of seven games over the Dodgers. But then two more pitchers were hurt, and the club lost eight straight.

Finally, it came down to one game. The Phils were closing the season at Ebbets Field against the Dodgers and had just a one-game lead. It was Newcombe against Roberts, both gunning for their 20th victories. Roberts was making his third start in five days and had to be arm-weary. Yet the two pitchers were brilliant, and the game was a 1-1 tie going into the bottom of the ninth inning.

Then the Dodgers began to rally. They put runners on first and second with no one out. Duke Snider was up and promptly rapped a single to center. But Richie Ashburn, who was playing shallow, charged the ball and threw Cal Abrams out at the plate. Then Furillo fouled out, Hodges flied out and the game went into extra innings.

**Opposite:** Righthander Robin Roberts won 20 games for the 1950 "Whiz Kids" of Philadelphia.

**Top right:** The Yankees' Whitey Ford pitching to Ed Waitkus of the Philadelphia Phillies in the 1950 Series.

**Above:** Whitey Ford as a rookie in 1950. The lefty came to the Yanks in mid-season and had a 9-1 record.

In the tenth Dick Sisler became the hero. The son of Hall of Famer George Sisler, he belted a three-run homer to sew up the pennant for the Phils and make Roberts a 20-game winner. Now the Whiz Kids had the unenviable task of meeting the Yankees in the World Series.

Despite their talent, the Yanks hadn't had an easy time of it in the season. They were chased all year by the Tigers, Red Sox and Indians. But the Bombers finally prevailed, wrapping it up in the final week and finishing three games on top of the Tigers. DiMaggio was slowing down, age and injuries taking their toll, yet the Yankee Clipper had managed 32 homers and 122 RBIs to go with his .301 batting average.

The real star was shortstop Rizzuto, who had had his finest season, with a .324 batting average and an MVP prize. Raschi had won 21, Lopat 18 and Reynolds 16, but a shot in the arm came from young lefthander Whitey Ford, who had compiled a 9-1 record after coming up from Kansas City in mid-season.

As it turned out, the Series was short and sweet . . . though not for the Whiz Kids. Because Roberts was still tired, MVP Konstanty got the start in the opener against Vic Raschi. Konstanty pitched brilliantly, but Raschi was just a shade better, and the Yanks made a fourth-inning run

**Above:** This four-frame batting sequence shows the powerful stroke of Pittsburgh's home run king, Ralph Kiner, a seven-time league leader.

**Left:** Big Walt Dropo was the AL Rookie of the Year in 1950. The Red Sox slugger clubbed 34 homers and drove home 144 runs.

**Opposite top:** Cleveland slugger Al Rosen led the AL with 37 homers in 1950. Three years later he was the league's MVP.

**Opposite below:** George Kell of Detroit was the AL batting champ in 1949 with a .343 mark. A year later he hit .340.

run scored on an error. The Yanks then won it in the ninth on a Jerry Coleman single to take a 3-0 lead in games. They completed the sweep a day later, winning 5-2 behind rookie Ford and Allie Reynolds. That made it two straight Series for Casey Stengel's Bronx Bombers.

There were other memorable baseball feats in 1950. Rookies of the Year were the Red Sox' slugging first baseman Walt Dropo in the American League and the Braves' quick center-fielder Sam Jethroe in the National. Dropo batted .322 and tied teammate Vern Stephens for the lead in RBIs, with 144. Jethroe, a black, hit .273 and led the league with 35 stolen bases.

The Braves' dynamic duo of Spahn and Sain joined Roberts as National League 20-game winners, while Cleveland's Bob Lemon and Vic Raschi turned the trick in the junior circuit. Batting champions were Musial again (.346) and Boston's Billy Goodman, who hit .354. Ralph Kiner repeated as NL homer champ, with 47, while the American League had a new king in Al Rosen of Cleveland, who clubbed 37. Del Ennis drove in 126 runs for the champion Phillies in the National, and George Kell of Detroit led the majors with 218 hits. On 31 August the Dodgers' Gil Hodges tied a major league record with four home runs in a game against the Braves at Ebbets Field. He was the first 20th century National Leaguer to belt a quartet of round-trippers in a single contest.

Baseball also experienced some losses in 1950. Grover Cleveland Alexander, one of the game's greatest pitchers, died on 4 November: it was Alexander who had last pitched the Phillies to a pennant in 1915. And in the American League an era of another kind ended. Connie Mack, the grand old man of baseball, announced his retirement as manager of the Philadelphia Athletics just two months shy of his 88th birthday.

Mack had managed the As for an incredible 50 consecutive years, since 1901, and had won nine pennants. Jimmy Dykes was his replacement, though Mack said he would remain as team president. During all his years on the bench, and through a number of different eras, Connie Mack never donned a baseball uniform. He managed wearing a suit and tie, like a true gentleman. He was one of a kind, a great pioneer who would live on to the ripe old age of 93. There would never be another like him.

Connie Mack was leaving a game that was beginning to enter its modern era. There were some great new superstars on the horizon, players who would dazzle the fans and set great records during their careers. And there was also a superteam that would dominate the game for more than another decade.

stand up for a 1-0 victory. A day later Reynolds defeated Roberts 2-1, DiMaggio being the hero with a dramatic 10th inning home run.

In the third game the Phils' Ken Heintzelman held a 2-1 lead over Eddie Lopat going into eighth inning at Yankee Stadium. But with two out, a trio of walks loaded the bases, and the tying

# CHAPTER V
# RIDING THE SUBWAY

A 1951 shot of Joe DiMaggio (l),
Mickey Mantle and Ted
Williams (r).

Mention 1951 to any baseball fan and the images are almost immediate. There were the debuts of two great young ballplayers and the retirement of a veteran superstar. There was a new baseball commissioner, and there was a midget who was used as a pinch hitter. There was an incredible pennant race, and there was a dramatic home run known to this day as "the shot heard round the world." And perhaps best of all, at least for New Yorkers, there was another Subway Series.

The New York Yankees had never been a team to stand pat. Once the ballclub began to really hit its stride in the mid-1920s the parade of talent just seemed to keep coming. And as a consequence, the Yanks became the most successful franchise in baseball history. They had a continuous succession of great players at nearly every position, but in addition to that luxury they always seemed to have a superstar, a player almost larger than life, a kind of living legend who symbolized the team and its success.

The superstar run began with the one and only Babe Ruth. His exploits need no explanation. While the Babe was still in his prime and belting the ball all over the lot, the Bombers came up with another extra great one, Lou Gehrig, the Iron Horse, considered one of the best ever. Ruth and Gehrig were a two-man wrecking crew until the aging Babe left the team. Then Gehrig carried on alone until he was joined by a graceful centerfielder from California named Joe DiMaggio. When Gehrig's career was ended by the onset of the illness that would take his life, DiMaggio carried on, propelling the Yankees to more pennants and world championships in the 1940s. But as the decade turned, it was obvious that DiMag was slowing down, and although no one knew it at the outset of the 1951 season, the Yankee Clipper was entering his last campaign: he would hang up the spikes after the season ended. Yet the line of Yankee superstars wouldn't end, for the next one was already waiting in the wings. His name: Mickey Charles Mantle.

Born in Spavinaw, Oklahoma, on 20 October 1931, Mickey Mantle grew up in a baseball-oriented atmosphere. His father, Elven "Mutt" Mantle, loved the game and taught his son the fundamentals early. He even named the boy after his favorite player, Hall of Fame catcher Mickey Cochrane. The elder Mantle was also the one who insisted that the youngster work on being a switch hitter, a move that would later pay big dividends.

Young Mickey grew up to be big, strong and fast. He was a high school football player as well as a baseball star. Kicked in the leg during a football game, he developed osteomyelitis, a bone in-

**Above:** Babe Ruth gets handshake from Lou Gehrig after his record 60th homer in 1927.

**Left:** In 1951 rookie Mickey Mantle became heir to the Ruth-Gehrig-DiMag tradition.

**Opposite:** Lou Gehrig, The Yankees' Iron Horse, was the man to whom Mantle was often compared.

players in camp. There was infielder Gil McDougald, another powerful young outfielder named Jackie Jensen and a brash young second baseman named Alfred Manual Martin, whom everyone called Billy.

But it was Mickey Mantle who was making the biggest impression with his incredibly long drives. The situation became even more dramatic when DiMaggio announced during the spring that this would be his last season. Maybe even Joe D had seen the handwriting on the ball: his logical successor was already there.

One other factor came into play during 1951. The conflict in Korea was entering its second year, and many ballplayers were again being drafted into the army. The Yanks had lost their brilliant young pitcher, Whitey Ford, for two years, and other young players had to spend time with Uncle Sam. Mantle, to the surprise of many, was turned down, deemed 4F. It was the osteomyelitis from years before. But many fans couldn't understand how such a powerful looking young man could be 4F, and Mantle had to bear the burnden of criticism from many disgruntled fans during those war years.

Otherwise, it was business as usual for the Yanks. There would be a challenge from Cleveland, with veteran Bob Feller having the final great season of his career, but the Yanks had just

fection that would have lingering affects in the later years of an injury-plagued career.

But when healthy, young Mantle could blast the ball a country mile from either side of the plate, and it wasn't long before his reputation began to spread. A pitcher-shortstop then, Mantle was first brought to the attention of Yankee scout Tom Greenwade when the youngster wasn't quite 16. Greenwade wasn't interested then, but a year later he was back. Mantle had gained 20 pounds and was hitting the baseball even harder. It didn't take the veteran scout long to realize the potential in the youngster's powerful body. After a talk with the rest of the family Greenwade signed the youngster, and Mickey Mantle began his professional career with Independence of the K-O-M League in 1949. He was just 17 years old.

A year later the young switcher hitter was at Joplin, where he tore up the league. He was still a shortstop then, but no one worried about his shaky fielding. That's because he hit a league-leading .383, with 26 homers and 136 RBIs. And when the Yanks played the Phillies in the 1950 World Series, Tom Greenwade was in attendance. All he talked about to anyone who would listen was Mickey Mantle.

When the Yanks came to spring training in 1951 they had a number of good young ball-

**Top left:** Joe DiMaggio announces his retirement following the 1951 season.

**Above:** Bob Feller of the Indians was still going strong in 1951.

too much firepower. The Bombers opened the year with rookie McDougald at third, young Jensen in left and rookie Mantle in right. DiMaggio as usual, was between them in center. They still had the big three of Reynolds, Raschi and Lopat, and a rookie righthander named Tom Morgan stepped into Ford's spot.

It was Jensen who stole the thunder in that first game, with a triple and homer off Boston lefty Bill Wight, but Mantle also got his first big league hit, a single in the sixth inning. Later in the year, when the pitchers found a couple of weak spots, Mantle would be sent to Kansas City for 40 games, then he would be brought back up to finish the year. But there wasn't anyone who didn't see the awesome potential of his talent.

While the Yankees were en route to another American League pennant the lowly St Louis Browns were once again languishing in the American League basement. Colorful owner Bill Veeck, never one to allow the game to become dull, decided to add a little something to his team in August. The Browns were hosting the Tigers in a doubleheader on 9 August when, in the bottom of the first inning of the second game, the Browns sent a pinch hitter up for leadoff man Frank Saucier.

The more than 18,000 fans on hand couldn't believe their eyes. The pinch hitter looked like a little boy. In reality, he was Eddie Gaedel, a 26-year-old midget, who stood just three feet, seven inches tall and weighed only 65 pounds. Seeing the player with the number 1/8 on his back come up to the plate, umpire Ed Hurley called time and demanded an explanation. Browns' manager Zack Taylor came out and showed umpire Hurley Gaedel's major league contract. The ump checked it out and then had no choice but to allow Gaedel to hit.

Facing Detroit righthander Bob Cain, Gaedel went into a crouch, leaving Cain almost no target. Sure enough, Cain walked him on four pitches, and when Gaedel reached first Jim Delsing went in to pinch run for him. No one would ever know if Veeck would have continued to use Gaedel in situations where he needed a walk, for the next day American League President Will Harridge decided not to approve Gaedel's playing contract, saying that to have Gaedel continue with the team would be "conduct detrimental to baseball."

That was to be the end of Eddie Gaedel's major league baseball career. He would complain that Harridge's ruling was unfair to little people, but it held. And later, looking back at what must have been a dream, Gaedel told friends: "I felt like Babe Ruth when I walked out on the field that day."

But back to baseball.

The Yanks continued to stay a couple of hops in front of the Indians. One of their outstanding pitchers, Allie Reynolds, really made news when he threw a pair of no-hit ballgames during the season. His first came on 12 July, against the rival Indians, Reynolds winning a 1-0 decision on a home run by Gene Woodling. and his second gem occurred on 28 September, when he blanked Boston 8-0 in a game that clinched the American League pennant for the Bombers.

In another year the arrival of a Mickey Mantle, the pair of no-hitters by Reynolds and the pinch-

**Above:** Mickey Mantle slams a basehit in his first Yankee game in April, 1951. The slugging switchhitter became famous wearing number 7, but as a rookie he wore number 6.

hit appearance by Eddie Gaedel might have really captured all the headlines. But in 1951 events in the National League also made baseball history. The New York Giants also had a rookie player that year, one who would not only rival Mantle for headlines in New York, but would be compared with him for years to come.

His name was Willie Howard Mays, and, like Mantle, he was a young ballplayer of almost unlimited potential, a player who could do it all. Born in Westfield, Alabama, on 6 May 1931, Willie Mays was the son of a man who spent some time with Birmingham Barons in the negro leagues. But because of Branch Rickey and Jackie Robinson, the younger Mays would have a chance to show his stuff in the majors. And that had always been his dream. As a youngster, whenever he left the house and his mother asked him where he was going, Willie Mays always gave the same answer: he was going to play ball. By the time he was 16 his multiple skills labeled him a future star, and when he was 19 the New York Giants had signed him to a contract. At that time Mays probably would have played the game for nothing.

Mays spent the 1950 season at Trenton and batted .353 in just 81 games. Then, at the outset of the 1951 campaign, the Giants assigned him to their top farm club at Minneapolis, where they could watch his development closely. What they saw was a young player tearing up the league. He

**Above left:** Browns manager Zack Taylor laces the shoe of midget Eddie Gaedel, who was hired to play one 1951 game as a publicity stunt.

**Left:** Allie "Superchief" Reynolds pitched for both the Indians and Yanks. In six Series he won seven and lost two, for a .778 mark.

**Opposite:** Yankee teammates set to congratulate Gene Woodling after his leadoff homer in the fifth game of the 1953 World Series.

**Opposite above:** Bobby Thomson of the Giants looks relaxed here. But his pennant-winning homer in 1951 caused as much excitement as there has ever been in baseball.

**Opposite below:** Jackie Robinson playing second base for Brooklyn.

**Top:** Giants' Manager Leo Durocher gives some advice to rookie Willie Mays 1951.

**Above:** Manager Charlie Dressen celebrates his first day as the Dodgers' manager in 1951.

Snider, Hodges and Robinson were all busting the baseball, and Roy Campanella was playing at a pace that would bring him the first of three Most Valuable Player awards.

The Giants also had a strong nucleus that year. A trade with the Braves had brought them Alvin Dark and Eddie Stanky to play short and second. They were solid at the corners, with Whitey Lockman at first and Bobby Thomson at third. Monte Irvin was having a great year, and Don Mueller was a strong hitter in right. Wes Westrum, while not as good a hitter as Berra and Campanella, was in their class as a receiver and handler of pitchers. Sal Maglie, back from the Mexican League, was the ace of a good pitching staff that also featured Larry Jansen, Jim Hearn and Dave Koslo. But there was still a missing ingredient. This was evident when the Giants started the season by losing 11 of their first 12 games. At first the team looked to make a trade. When nothing materialized, it looked to the farm. And there was Willie Mays, hitting an incredible .477 after 35 games, with 71 hits in 149 trips to the plate. He was five hits short of batting .500. It didn't take Leo Durocher long to see the light. "Get Mays up here," he roared.

The Giants did. The rookie reported in late May, and from the moment he arrived Manager Durocher took him under his wing. The youngster wasn't used to the big city, and he was nervous. And when he went hitless in his first 12 at bats he told his manager that he thought he should return to the minors. "Nonsense," Durocher told him. "Stop worrying. Even if you don't get a hit in fifty at bats, you're still my centerfielder. And don't forget that."

did everything with a dash and flair that hadn't been seen in years. He could hit for both average and power, could run, steal bases and throw. In centerfield he was a marvel. He caught fly balls with his glove at his waist, a "basket" catch that most baseball people would frown upon. But with Willie Mays it seemed natural. When he went after a ball, always with exquisite timing, his cap would invariably fly off his head, giving his pursuit even more drama.

While the Giants were watching their phenom perform at Minneapolis they were also watching the Dodgers take off like a rocket, seemingly intent on making the National League race a shambles by the Fourth of July. Brooklyn was operating under new manager Charlie Dressen, and all their great stars were really rolling.

The next night Mays got his first big league hit, a long home run off Boston's great lefty, Warren Spahn. It still took him a while to settle in, but once he did he really began to contribute to the Giants' effort, and the New Yorkers began to gain ground on the arch-rival Dodgers. It was to turn into one of the great pennant chases in baseball history.

By the middle of August the Dodgers still had what seemed an insurmountable lead. They were 13½ games ahead of the second-place Giants. But then the Jints began to click, reeling off a streak of 16 consecutive victories. At the same time, the Dodgers began playing poorly for the first time all year. Brooklyn lost nine of 18, and their lead had shrunk to just 5½ games by 9 September. Now there was a real pennant race.

The Giants kept rolling. They won 16 of their final 20 games, slowly closing the gap, for the Dodgers had suddenly become a .500 team. When the Giants won on the final day of the season, they took a ½ game lead over the Dodgers, who were then playing at Philadelphia.

At one point the Phillies had a 6-1 lead, but the Dodgers rallied to tie the game and it went into extra innings. Then, in the bottom of the 12th, the Phils loaded the bases with two out, and Eddie Waitkus hit a shot to the right of second baseman Robinson. At first it looked like the game-winning and pennant-deciding hit. But Robinson dove headfirst for the ball and caught it backhanded just before it hit the ground and went past him. Robby fell so hard that he was actually knocked unconscious for a few seconds. But he held the ball. Two innings later Robinson was a hero once more when he belted a two-run homer to win the game for the Dodgers.

Both the Dodgers and the Giants had finished with identical 96-58 records and would have to play a best-of-three playoff series to decide the National League champion. With the Yanks having won the American League flag by five games, New York fans were not only guaranteed a Subway Series, but a Subway Playoff as well. Yet no one could have predicted the incredible moment that was about to take place.

The first playoff game was played at Ebbets Field in Brooklyn, and the Giants won it 3-1 behind big Jim Hearn. In that game the Giants' Bobby Thomson homered off Dodger pitcher Ralph Branca. Then, with the series shifting back to the Polo Grounds, the Dodgers bounced back. With surprise starter Clem Labine pitching brilliantly the Dodgers won easily, 10-0, setting up a third and decisive game at the Polo Grounds, with the pennant the prize.

Behind the pitching of Big Don Newcombe the Dodgers took a 4-1 lead and still held it going into the bottom of the ninth inning. The Giants

**Top:** Lines show flight of Bobby Thomson's historic home run off Ralph Branca.

**Above:** Thomson celebrates with Manager Durocher (r) and Giants owner Horace Stoneham after the game.

were now three outs away from seeing their courageous comeback fall a game short. But when Alvin Dark led off the inning with a basehit, there was a flicker of hope. Don Mueller followed with another single, putting two runners on. Then Monte Irvin popped out and the fans at the Polo Grounds groaned. Only two outs left.

Whitey Lockman was next. He picked out a Newcombe fastball and whacked a double to left. Dark scored, with Mueller going to third. Unfortunately, Mueller broke his ankle sliding in and had to be removed from the game. But it was now 4-2, and while Mueller was being carried from the field Brooklyn skipper Charlie Dressen came out and gave Newcombe the hook. He brought in big Ralph Branca to pitch to the next hitter, Bobby Thomson.

So the stage was set. Thomson had 31 homers so far, and if he failed, the great rookie, Willie Mays, was on deck. Branca's first pitch was a fastball on the inside corner for a strike. Then, instead of coming outside, Branca threw a second fastball to the same spot. But Thomson wasn't fooled. He hit a rising line drive into the left field stands for a game- and pennant-winning three-run homer, perhaps the most dramatic in baseball history.

As Thomson circled the bases and the Giants gathered at home plate in jubiliation, announcer Russ Hodges repeated over and over again to the huge television audience: "The Giants win the pennant, the Giants win the pennant, the Giants win the pennant. . . !"

It was an incredible end to an extraordinary season. Mays wound up with 20 home runs, 68 RBIs and a .274 batting average in his first sea-

**Left:** Rookie Gil McDougald flashes across home with the Yanks' only run in the 1951 Series opener. The on-deck hitter is Joe Collins, and the Giants' catcher is Wes Westrum.

**Below:** Stan Musial smiles after getting a silver bat from NL President Warren Giles. The prize was given for Stan The Man's fifth batting title, which he won in 1951 with a .355 average.

son, good enough to win the Rookie of the Year prize. Mantle, who had returned from his trip to the minors to finish strongly, hit .267, with 13 homers and 65 runs batted in for 96 games. The Rookie of the Year in the AL was his teammate, Gil McDougald, who batted .306. And in his final season Joe DiMaggio hit .263, with 12 homers and 71 ribbys. He finished his great career with a .325 lifetime average, 361 home runs, his record-breaking 56-game hitting streak and some great memories for everyone who ever saw him.

The batting champs in 1951 were Musial once again in the NL, with a .355 mark, and the As' Ferris Fain in the AL, at .344. Ralph Kiner, with 42, and Gus Zernial, with 33, were the homer kings, while Monte Irvin, with 121 RBIs, led the National, and Gus Zernial, with 129, the American. Richie Ashburn (221) and George Kell (191) had the most hits, while Sam Jethroe, with 35, and Minnie Minoso, with 31, topped the respective leagues in steals.

It was also a great year for pitchers. Maglie and Jansen of the Giants won 23 games each, the Dodgers' Preacher Roe was an amazing 22-3, while teammate Don Newcombe went 20-9. Spahn won 22, Robin Roberts 21 and Murray Dickson of the Pirates 20. In the American

League Feller was the top winner, with a 22-8 record, followed by Lopat and Raschi, with 21 wins each. Early Wynn and Mike Garcia of Cleveland each won 20 to back up Feller, and Ned Garver of St Louis also become a 20-game winner for the first time. The Yanks' Reynolds, who pitched the two no-hitters, finished at 17-8. And when the smoke from the season cleared, the two great catchers, Berra and Campanella, would walk away with their league's Most Valuable Player prizes. When the World Series finally began baseball also had a new Commissioner. Ford C Frick had been elected to replace "Happy" Chandler as baseball's third czar.

Now it was time for New York fans to jump the subways again. Durocher's Giants would have to play the Series without Don Mueller, a solid hitter, while the Yanks would lose Mickey Mantle in game two when he would injure a knee after stepping on a water drain in the Yankee Stadium outfield, an injury that would require surgery.

Because he felt both Jensen and Maglie were tired from the pennant chase and playoffs, Durocher started lefty Dave Koslo in game one, and he surprised the Yanks by throwing a seven-hitter and defeating Allie Reynolds 5-1. Monte

Irvin had four hits, and Al Dark a homer for the Giants.

The Yanks got even in game two, winning 3-1 behind Ed Lopat's five-hit pitching and a homer from first baseman Joe Collins. Now the Series moved to the Polo Grounds, where the Giants took a 2-1 lead in games as Jim Hearn defeated Vic Raschi 6-2. It was in this game that Eddie Stanky kicked the ball out of Phil Rizzuto's glove on a tag play at second. The maneuver helped pave the way for five Giants' runs and a 6-0 lead in the fifth inning.

But the Bronx Bombers turned the tables in game four, winning 6-2 as Allie Reynolds bested Sal Maglie. The highlight of this one was a homer by DiMaggio, his last in World Series play. A day later the Yanks banged out 12 hits en route to a 13-1 victory behind another Lopat five-hitter. Rookie Gil McDougald made history in this one by becoming the first rookie to hit a grand slam home run in World Series competition. Now the Yanks had a 3-2 lead, with Vic Raschi set to go against Dave Koslo in the sixth game.

The game was close until the sixth inning. With the score tied at 1-1 Yankee rightfielder

**Below:** Monte Irvin of the Giants stealing home in the opener of the 1951 World Series. The Yankee catcher is Yogi Berra, and the next hitter, Bobby Thomson, has fallen to get out of the way.

**Right:** The Giants' Eddie Stanky has just kicked the ball from Yankee shortstop Phil Rizzuto's glove in game three of '51 World Series. The Giants won 6-2.

**Right:** The Giants' Eddie Stanky has just kicked the ball from Yankee shortstop Phil Rizzuto's glove in game three of '51 World Series. The Giants won 6-2.

**Below:** Yankee southpaw Ed Lopat was on the mound as the Yanks won game five of the Series 13-1. Lopat threw a five-hitter, and rookie Gil McDougald belted a grand-slam homer.

Hank Bauer blasted a bases-loaded triple to give the Yanks a 4-1 lead. And when the Giants rallied in the ninth, loading the bases against reliever Johnny Sain, it was Bauer to the rescue once again.

With lefthander Bob Kuzava on the mound the Giants got a pair of runs on fly balls to left. Then, with two out, pinch hitter Sal Yvars hit a sinking liner to right. Bauer raced in and made a sliding catch for a third out that ended the Series and made the Yankees champions for a third consecutive year.

Irvin led all batters, with 11 hits and a .458 average, while Dark had 10 safeties and a .417 mark. Bobby Brown hit .357, and Rizzuto .320 for the Yanks. And while he hit just .261, Joe DiMaggio had a double in game six. It would be his final at bat in the big leagues and a fitting way to end both his career and another great season for the Yanks.

There was a great deal of talk about dynasty when 1952 rolled around. And in the next two years Casey Stengel and the Yankees would come as close as any team ever did to complete domination of a sport. But as the new season began there was still much concern about the continuing war in Korea. The draft was widening and more players were having to give their time to the service.

The Yanks had already lost Whitey Ford the year before and would again be without the stylish lefthander in 1952. Infielder Jerry Coleman had been a fighter pilot in World War II and was now recalled to active duty. Another infielder, Bobby Brown, also went, as did pitcher Tom Morgan. And at the end of April it was announced that Ted Williams, also a former fighter pilot, was being recalled to active duty. Williams blasted a game-winning two-run homer against Washington in his final game before leaving.

In the National League the Giants had gotten off to a fast start in 1952, hoping to defend their National League crown. Then, in May, the team got the bad news. Willie Mays was being inducted into the service and would be leaving on 29 May. The loss of Mays for two years would really be felt by the Jints. They just weren't the same team without the Say Hey Kid.

The loss of Mays to the service made it even more difficult for his crosstown counterpart, Mickey Mantle. Examined by his draft board once more, Mickey was again declared unfit for service. He still had the history of osteomyelitis and was coming off knee surgery, but the average fan still saw him as a young, strong powerhouse who could hit, run and throw as well as anyone. He heard plenty of catcalls coming from the stands in ballparks all around the league during this period.

The Dodgers weren't left untouched either, for they lost Don Newcombe, who had won 20 games in 1951. Big Newk would also give two years to the military before returning in 1954. Fortunately for the Brooks, however, they came up with a strong-armed righthanded relief pitcher, Joe Black, who would win 15 games and be named National League Rookie of the Year.

The Giants, too, came up with a relief pitcher who not only kept them in the 1952 race, but would also make his own personal mark on the game. His name was Hoyt Wilhelm, and in 1952 he made 71 appearances and finished with a 15-3 record. Wilhelm was unique in that despite being nearly 29 years old when he came to the majors, he would still pitch for 21 seasons and would retire at the ripe of age of 49, after having appeared in more major league games than any pitcher in history.

One reason for Wilhelm's durability was the knuckleball, a pitch he had perfected. The knuckler is unpredictable and difficult to hit (or catch, for that matter). It flutters up to home plate with little or no spin and can dip or sail in almost any direction. Because it's not thrown hard, the pitch puts little strain on the arm, and the knuckleballers – a rare breed – generally last a long time. Wilhelm spun his magic for nine different teams during his long career and eventually won 143 games. He also started on occasion and was good enough to throw a no-hitter against

**Opposite top:** Joe D, with his flawless batting style.

**Opposite bottom:** Stengel and Mantle share thoughts.

**Above:** DiMaggio slams a home run in his last World Series in 1951.

**Left:** McDougald heads for the dugout after his 1951 World Series grand slam.

**Left:** These five players formed the heart and soul of the Brooklyn Dodgers during the glory years of the 1950s. Left to right, Duke Snider, Gil Hodges, Jackie Robinson, Pee Wee Reese and Roy Campanella. All but Hodges have been elected to baseball's Hall of Fame.

the New York Yankees while pitching for the Baltimore Orioles in 1958.

Another pitcher who made his mark during the 1952 season was Bobby Shantz of the Philadelphia As. Just 5′ 6″, the little lefty had come up in 1949 and, pitching for a losing team in 1951, became a winner at 18-10. The next year, Shantz almost made the club respectable. He was the best pitcher in the American League, with a 24-7 record, led the usually lowly As to a 79-75 finish and won the Most Valuable Player Award. Though he hung on with several other teams until 1964, the little guy never again won 20 or came close to duplicating the magical year he had had in 1952.

It would be a good year for pitchers in the American League. In addition to Shantz, Cleveland's big three of Wynn, Lemon and Garcia would win 23, 22 and 22 games respectively, and New York's Allie Reynolds would also reach the 20-victory plateau. But in the senior circuit only one hurler would reach the magic 20-win circle. Yet he, too, created a bit of a stir.

He was Robin Roberts of the Phils, who for a time looked as though he might become the big leagues' first 30-game winner since Dizzy Dean turned the trick in 1934. Roberts came up a little short of 30, but turned in a brilliant 28-7 record, baseball's best overall pitching performance during 1952.

There were some other fine individual performances during the season. Veteran Cubs slugger Hank Sauer won the National League MVP prize by hitting .270, tying Ralph Kiner for the home run lead, with 37, and leading the league with 121 RBIs. Musial, at .336, and Fain, at .327, repeated their batting titles of a year earlier. Larry Doby became the first black to lead the American League in homers, with 32, and teammate Al Rosen led the league in ribbys, with 105. Musial and Nellie Fox of the White Sox led their respective leagues in hits, while Warren Spahn (183) and Allie Reynolds (160) were the top strikeout pitchers.

**Below:** Hank Sauer was a top slugger for the Reds, Cubs, Cards and Giants from 1941 to 1959.

But teamwise it was the Dodgers and the Yankees, though each had to battle for the flag. For the Yanks, it was the fourth American League pennant in a row. The Bombers finished at 95-59, beating out the Indians by a scant two games, while the Dodgers ended the season with a 96-57 record, topping the second place Giants by 4½.

Still, the Yanks had had to struggle a bit. Despite the fact that he had slipped noticeably the year before, the team still missed the presence of Joe DiMaggio. Mantle was coming on (a .311 average, 23 homers and 87 RBIs) but still had not achieved the status of the Yankee Clipper. In addition, Ed Lopat was slidelined part of the year with a bad shoulder and won just 10 games. And Vic Raschi dipped to 16 after three straight 21-game seasons. Young Billy Martin had taken over the Coleman at second, while aging John Mize split time with Joe Collinsat first. It wasn't the usual powerhouse Yankee team, but it was still formidable.

The loss of Newcombe to the army hurt the Dodgers. But Black filled part of the void and Erskine won 14, Roe 11 and young Billy Loes 13. So while the club might not have had a stopper on the mound, they weren't too badly off, and the likes of Robinson, Hodges, Snider, Campanella

and Furillo produced a lot of runs.

That put everyone back on the subway again and out to Ebbets Field for the first game of the World Series. Manager Chuck Dressen acknowledged his lack of pitching by going to Joe Black in game one. Black had been strictly a reliever until the final two weeks of the season. Now he was starting the biggest game of his life. The Yanks countered with their 20-game winner, Allie Reynolds.

**Above:** Joe Black was a standout reliever for the Dodgers in 1952. But when asked to start the first game of the World Series against the Yanks, he went all the way, for a 4-2 victory.

**Left:** Hoyt Wilhelm was close to 29 when he reached the majors in 1952. But his great knuckleball kept him in the bigs for 20 years and enabled him to pitch in a record 1070 games.

Home runs by Robinson and McDougald accounted for the early runs, but both pitchers were looking sharp. It was still 1-1 in the bottom of the sixth when Duke Snider smacked a two-run shot over the rightfield wall to make it a 3-1 game. The Yanks got a run of Black in the eighth to draw closer, but Pee Wee Reese surprised everyone with a solo shot off reliever Ray Scarborough in the bottom of the inning. The 4-2 final score gave Black the victory and the Dodgers a 1-0 lead in games.

The Yanks, however, were not a team to stay down long. Raschi got them even in game two, besting Erskine 7-1, with Billy Martin driving home four runs on two hits, including a homer. With the Series returning to Yankee Stadium, Ed Lopat hooked up with Preacher Roe in a battle of lefties in game three. It was another close one, the Dodgers holding a mere 2-1 lead going into the eighth inning. A Brooklyn run in the top of the frame made it 3-1, but the Bombers came right back in the bottom to make it 3-2.

Then, in the top of the ninth, Berra, who had homered earlier, became the goat. He allowed one of reliever Tom Gorman's pitches to slip past him, and two more Dodger runs scampered home, making it a 5-2 game. A solo shot by big John Mize in the bottom of the inning brought it to 5-3, but the Dodgers were up by a game once again.

With their backs getting closer to the wall in game four, the Yanks went back to their ace, Allie Reynolds, and he responded by outpitching Black and winning 2-0 on a four-hitter. John Mize had another homer in this one. Now came

first world championship ever. With the Series now back in Brooklyn, the Yanks sent Vic Raschi to the mound to face the Dodgers' Billy Loes. Once again the game was a tight one. It was scoreless until the bottom of the sixth, when the Dodgers pushed across a run on another homer by Duke Snider. But in the seventh Berra homered to tie it, then Woodling singled. He went to second on a balk and scored when Raschi's hit went off Loes' knee. That's when Loes made his classic statement about the grounder: "I lost it in the sun."

Mantle's long homer in the top of the eighth gave the Yanks an insurance run, which they needed, because Snider hit his second homer of the game and fourth of the Series in the bottom of the eighth. But the 3-2 victory enabled the Yanks to tie the Series once more. Now it was Lopat against Black in the seventh and deciding game.

Once again it was a tight and tense battle, as the entire Series had been. The Dodgers got single runs in the fourth and fifth, but the Yanks got tallies in the fourth, fifth, sixth and seventh to take a 4-2 victory, as Stengel juggled his players and used four different pitchers, including Reynolds and Raschi, to lead the Yanks to a fourth straight World Series triumph. Woodling and Mantle belted homers to help the Bomber cause. And once again Dodger fans rallied behind a cry that had seemingly become an annual ritual. "Wait till next year," they would tell anyone who'd listen.

Next year, 1953, began with an event that would eventually change the entire face of the game. The Boston Braves, one of the National League's original franchises, was picking up stakes. There had been a Boston team in the old National Association, which began keeping records in 1871, and the franchise had remained in Beantown when the National League was formed in 1876 and had stayed there right through the first half of the 20th century. But in March 1953 Braves owner Lou Perini suprised many people by announcing that the franchise was moving to Wisconsin, effective immediately, and would begin the new season as the Milwaukee Braves. It would be the first National League franchise shift in 53 years. The reason: sagging attendance. Only 281,000 fans had attended Braves' games in 1952, down from 1,455,439 just four years earlier, when the team had won the National League pennant. Perini said the ballclub had lost more than a half million dollars during the 1952 season.

The franchise shift would be watched with great interest by many other baseball people. For years major league franchises had been etched in stone. Now a team was moving to another city.

**Opposite below:** Dodger skipper Chuck Dressen (left) hugs pitcher Carl Erskine after "Oisk" topped the Braves 5-2 to clinch the 1953 pennant.

**Above:** The Yanks' Billy Martin races in to snare Jackie Robinson's pop fly with the bases loaded, thus saving the '52 Series for the Bombers.

the crucial fifth game, as Carl Erskine went to the mound against surprise starter Ewell Blackwell, whom the Yanks had picked up from Cincinnati late in the season.

It was a strange game. The Yanks got all five of their runs in the fifth inning, three of them riding home on another circuit shot by Mize. But the Dodgers chipped away for one in the second, three in the fifth and another in the seventh to tie it. Snider was the big gun, with a two-run homer in the fifth and a run-scoring single in the seventh. Erskine, meanwhile, had settled down and retired the last 19 Yanks in a row as the game went into the eleventh inning. That's when the Dodgers got the winning run, Snider again doing the damage with a double. The 6-5 final score new gave the Dodgers a 3-2 lead.

Brooklyn needed just a single victory to win its

And the move began paying dividends almost immediately. The first 13 home games at Milwaukee's County Stadium drew 302,667 fans, outstripping the Braves' entire attendence figure for 77 home games at Boston the year before. By the end of the year the Braves would set a new National League attendance record of more than 1,800,000 fans and would go over the two million mark a year later, the first of four successive two-million seasons at the gate. So successful was the Braves' move that it set a number of other owners to thinking strange new thoughts.

On the playing field it was again the Yankees and the Dodgers. The Bombers would roll to a fifth consecutive American League pennant, a new record, by beating out perennial runner-up Cleveland by 8½ games. In the National League the Dodgers did even better. With their great team continuing to mature, Brooklyn won 105 games and outdistanced runner-up Milwaukee by 13 full lengths. But the Braves, playing in their enthusiastic new city, had jumped from seventh to second, winning 28 more games than the old Boston Braves had won the year before.

It was an interesting year in other ways as well. Carl Furillo of the Dodgers was the new National League batting champ, with a .344 mark, edging out the Cards' Red Schoendienst, who hit .342, and Musial, who hit "only" .337. Young Eddie Mathews of the Braves, in just his second full season and barely 22-years-old, clubbed 47 homers to end Ralph Kiner's seven-year reign as National League home run king.

562 FEET

**Opposite top:** Dodger star Carl Erskine en route to a no-hitter against the Cubs in June 1952.

**Opposite below:** One of the best second baseman of his time, Al "Red" Schoendienst.

**Above:** A diagram of Mickey Mantle's mammoth homer in Griffith Stadium.

**Right:** Harvey Kuenn of Detroit was the American League Rookie of the Year in 1953.

Roy Campanella of the Dodgers, in what would be another Most Valuable Player season, batted .312, hit 41 homers and drove in a league-leading 142 runs. Jim "Junior" Gilliam of the Dodgers was the Rookie of the Year. A slick second baseman, Gilliam's presence allowed the Dodgers to move the aging Robinson to third base and the outfield. There were also a couple of familiar names in the 20-win circle, as Warren Spahn and Robin Roberts each won 23 times. The Dodgers' Carl Erskine and Harvey Haddix of St Louis won 20 apiece.

In the American League there were also four 20-game winners, led by Bob Porterfield of Washington, with 22. Mel Parnell of Boston and Bob Lemon of Cleveland won 21, while Virgil "Fire" Trucks of the White Sox copped 20. The year before, Trucks had thrown a pair of no-hitters for the Tigers yet had compiled only a 5-19 record.

Mickey Vernon of Washington took his second American League batting title, with a .337 mark, while Al Rosen regained the home run crown from Cleveland teammate Larry Doby by hitting 43. Rosen also led the junior circuit with 145 RBIs and was named the league MVP. A young Detroit shortstop named Harvey Kuenn led the league in hitting, with 209, compiled a batting average of .308 and was named Rookie of the Year.

One of the big events of the year was the return of Ted Williams from active duty in Korea. The Splendid Splinter came back a hero after he safely landed his flaming jet by skidding 2000 feet along a runaway with no landing gear and, as one writer said, with death as his co-pilot.

The war experience had had a sobering effect on the Splinter, who also suffered some hearing loss from the concussive effects of bombs and gunfire. At 35 he was undecided about returning to baseball. What changed his mind was an accidental meeting with the Mahatma, Branch Rickey, at an airport. The usually candid Rickey didn't mince words. "Ted, you've got five or six more good years left," he told the Splinter. "I think you should play."

Williams took about ten days of batting practice, then pinch hit in a game at Washington on 6 August and popped out. But three days later he pinch hit in Boston against Cleveland's Mike Garcia and blasted a home run into the far reaches of Fenway Park. Ted was back. In the final 37 games of the season he batted .407, smacked 13 homers and drove home 34 runs. His slugging percentage was an incredible .901, but then Ted Williams was never a batter to whom ordinary standards could be applied.

Though the Yanks didn't have a statistical leader or a 20-game winner, they won their fifth straight easily. At one point the club had an 18-game win streak. Mantle had 21 homers and 92 RBIs, while catcher Berra clubbed 27 round-trippers and drove home 108. And they got the usual support from the likes of Bauer, Woodling, McDougald, Collins, Rizzuto and Martin.

Although the Big Three of Reynolds, Raschi and Lopat was beginning to age, young Whitey Ford had come out of the army to become the ace of the staff, with an 18-6 record. Reynolds, a year away from retirement, won 13, as did Raschi,

who would be traded the following season. Lopat won 16 but would have just one more better-than-average season. So the face of the team was starting to change.

The Dodgers, however, seemed at a peak. Furillo was the batting champ, and Campy the MVP. Robinson hit .329 and drove in 95 runs. Duke Snider and Gil Hodges were both fence busters. Reese was still an anchor at short, and now the team had added Gilliam. Only the pitching was a question mark, even though the team won 105 games. With Newcombe still in the service, Erskine was the ace at 20-6, Roe was 11-3, Loes 14-8, Labine 11-6, Black 6-3 and Russ Meyer a surprise at 15-5. So, collectively, they got the job done.

But could they do it against the seemingly invincible Yankees? By now some people felt the Dodgers were jinxed. Not only had the team never won a World Series, they had been beaten by the rival Yanks in 1941, 1947, 1949 and 1952.

The 1953 Series opened at Yankee Stadium with the Bombers sending Allie Reynolds to the mound against the Dodgers' Carl Erskine. And it

**Opposite:** Brooklyn's Carl Erskine shown chalking up the number of strikeouts he threw against the Yanks in game three of the 1953 World Series.

**Below:** The Dodgers' 1953 infield featured, l to r, Gil Hodges, Junior Gilliam, Pee Wee Reese and Jackie Robinson.

**Below:** This happy quartet of Yankees are celebrating their 9-5 opening-game win in the 1953 World Series. From left are Hank Bauer, Yogi Berra, Billy Martin and Joe Collins.

didn't take the Yanks long to send the Dodgers a message. They scored four first-inning runs, driving the Brooklyn righty to the showers, and then held on for a 9-5 victory, even though the Dodgers had come back to tie the game in the top of the seventh. Billy Martin had three hits for the Yanks, while Gil Hodges did the same for Brooklyn. There were also five homers hit in the fray.

It settled down a bit the next day. Eddie Lopat quieted the Brooklyn bats as the Yanks got one in the seventh and two in the eighth to win 4-2. Billy Martin belted the tying home run off Preacher Roe in the seventh, and a two-run shot by the mighty Mantle in the eighth proved the game-winner. With the series returning to Brooklyn, the Dodgers were down two games and in trouble.

Because he had only pitched one inning of the first game, Carl Erskine was manager Dressen's choice in game three, opposing veteran Yankee Vic Raschi. It was a different Erskine in this one. Though the game was close, the Dodgers won it 3-2. "Oisk" was in command all the way, setting a World Series record with 14 strikeouts, including Mickey Mantle and Joe Collins four times each. He had pitched the Dodgers back into it.

The next day they tied it up. Billy Loes started against the Yanks' Whitey Ford, and the Dodgers jumped on the young lefty for three first-inning runs en route to a 7-3 victory. Snider, with a homer, two doubles and four RBIs, led the Dodger 12-hit attack.

Jim McDonald, a 9-7 pitcher during the regular season, was a surprise starter for the Yanks in the pivotal fifth game, while the Dodgers went with young Johnny Podres. This one was a slugfest in which the Dodgers outhit the Yanks 14-11, yet still lost the game 11-7. A third-inning grand slam homer by Mantle off reliever Russ Meyer broke the game open. And true to their name, the Bronx Bombers hit three more circuit shots – by Woodling, Martin and McDougald – to take a 3-2 lead in games.

With the Series back at Yankee Stadium, Whitey Ford went for the clincher against Carl Erskine. The Yanks jumped on top 3-0 at the end of two. But the Dodgers clawed back and tied the game in dramatic fashion in the ninth. With Brooklyn trailing 3-1, and facing Allie Reynolds, Carl Furillo hit a two-run homer to knot the ballgame and hopefully save the Dodgers from defeat.

Then, with Clem Labine pitching in the last of the ninth, Hank Bauer walked. After Berra lined out, Mantle used his great speed to leg out an infield hit. Finally, Billy Martin lashed a single to center to drive in Bauer with the championship run. The Yanks had done it again.

The Dodgers had actually outhit the Yanks as a team, batting an even .300 for the Series, while the Yanks checked in at .279. But Billy Martin, who hit just .257 during the regular season, set a record by getting 12 hits in six games. Billy the Kid batted .500, with a double, triple, two homers and eight RBIs. Berra was behind him at .429, and Mantle drove in seven runs with a pair of homers.

Gil Hodges led the Dodgers, with a .364 mark, followed by Furillo at .333, Snider and Robinson at .320, Cox at .304, Gilliam at .296 and Campanella at .273. So almost all of the Dodger stars had hit very well, but the Yanks had still won in six. Maybe the superstitious were right and the Dodgers were jinxed after all.

The Yankees had racked up five straight World Series triumphs under Casey Stengel, affirming their position as baseball's reigning dynasty. And since the Dodgers and Giants were the two best teams in the National League, four of the five World Series had been played exclusively in New York, while the clattering subways carried delirious fans back and forth from Yankee Stadium to the Polo Grounds and Ebbets Field.

# CHAPTER VI
# THE OLD
# AND
# THE NEW

Vice-President Richard M Nixon throws out first ball of 1954 season.

There's an old cliche that says the more things change the more they stay the same. It's an adage that aptly applies to the years of the middle 1950s. The face of the game was changing, with many bright new players coming into the Bigs and a number of franchise shifts. But it also stayed the same in that the New York Yankees continued to be baseball's dominant team. They would be challenged, however, first by their old nemesis, the Dodgers, and then by a new kid on the block, the Milwaukee Braves. But before that happened the Yanks and Dodgers had to take a year off. In 1954 both would fail to repeat as champs in their respective leagues.

When the 1954 season opened the American League had a new look. The struggling St Louis Browns had been sold, then moved soon after the 1953 season ended. When 1954 arrived the fran-

**Right:** Young Henry Aaron.

**Below:** Young Al Kaline.

chise was in Baltimore, and the team known as the Orioles. It was also the year in which Willie Mays would return from two years in the service and a couple of National League rookies would ease onto the scene, not much noticed at first, but both beginning long, record-breaking careers that would eventually land them in baseball's Hall of Fame.

One of the rookies was a Chicago Cubs shortstop named Ernie Banks. He was a thin black man with quick wrists and an explosive bat. Once he got going, Banks would become a home run king and a two-time Most Valuable Player who would hit more than 500 home runs over a long career, more than any other shortstop who ever played the game. And along with his ability, his attitude toward baseball was great. Banks never had a bad word for anyone and he loved the game. Playing in the daytime sun of Chicago's lightless Wrigley Field, Banks was often heard to say, "It's a beautiful day. Let's play two!"

The other rookie was a 20-year-old outfielder for the Milwaukee Braves named Henry Louis Aaron. It wouldn't be long before he would be known as "Hammerin' Hank," and later, "Bad Henry." But Bad Henry was good. Oh, was he good. And before he was through he would become baseball's all time home run king, as well as the game's all-time best in a number of other hitting categories.

Aaron was born in Mobile, Alabama, on 5

February 1934, and was yet another example of a young southern black who, just 10 years earlier, wouldn't have been able to begin his career in the major leagues. But thanks to Jackie Robinson, a Hank Aaron could now come to the majors at 20 and become a legend.

While he didn't play with the same style and flair of Willie Mays, and he didn't hit the high, long, majestic home runs of Mickey Mantle, Aaron was quietly efficient in every phase of the game. He was also incredibly consistent. That's why it took him ten years or more to get the wide-spread recognition accorded the other two much sooner. But Aaron definitely joined with Mays and Mantle as the reigning triumvirate of super stars in the 1950s and 1960s, just as DiMaggio, Musial and Williams had been in the era directly preceding. To be sure, the last two were still going strong, since baseball "eras" generally overlap.

**Above:** Ace shortstop Ernie Banks of the Cubs would be a two-time MVP in the 1950s and would hit more than 500 home runs to earn a place in baseball's Hall of Fame.

**Left:** Back from the army, Willie Mays had a great 1954 season. But here he is tagged out at the plate by Cardinal catcher Bill Sarni.

**Below:** Burly Early Wynn was part of the great Cleveland pitching staff that helped the tribe to a record 111 victories in 1954. Wynn won 23 of them.

The American League also had a rookie that year who would become one of the finer players in the game. He was Al Kaline, an outfielder with the Detroit Tigers who had made his debut the year before at the age of 18. He would play 138 games in 1954, hitting .276. A year later, however, he would really hit his stride and everyone in baseball would know about Al Kaline.

With so many young players coming into both leagues, and others like Mantle and Mays really beginning to establish themselves, the game was obviously changing. But some things never seemed to change. Ted Williams would hit .345, with 29 homers and 89 RBIs in just 117 games, while Musial banged away at .330, with 35 homers and 126 RBIs. What consistently great ballplayers the two of them were.

The pennant races of 1954 proved something of a surprise. The Yanks, led by Mantle, Berra and Whitey Ford, would be better than ever. Berra, in fact, would be the American League's Most Valuable Player for a second time, with an outstanding season in which he would bat .307, club 22 homers and drive home 125 runs. The team would win 103 games, more than they had won in any of their five previous pennant seasons. They also had the Rookie of the Year in pitcher Bob Grim, who went 20-6. But despite all this, they wouldn't finish first.

That was because the Cleveland Indians, under the wily leadership of Al Lopez, put together one of the finest seasons of modern times. The Indians always had the great pitching from the likes of Lemon, Wynn, Garcia and the aging Feller. And they had some power with Al Rosen

**Left:** Batting champ Bobby Avila (left) and slugger Al Rosen both played big roles in Cleveland's great 1954 season.

**Below:** This is the hitting style that took Willie Mays to the 1954 National League batting title with a .345 average.

and Larry Doby. But they always seemed to fall just short of the Yanks. In 1954, however, they put it all together and wiped up the Yanks and all the rest of the American League.

The Indians won 111 games and lost just 43, breaking the league record of 110 victories set by the great 1927 Yankees. That gave them the American League flag by a comfortable eight games. And they did it with some really outstanding individual performances, beginning with their pitching staff.

Bob Lemon checked in with a 23-7 record, while burly Early Wynn finished 23-11. Mike Garcia had a 19-8 mark, and the great Bob Feller, made a spot starter at age 35, was 13-3. The staff was even more formidable due to the presence of a pair of rookie relievers. Lefty Don Mossi was 6-1 in 40 games, while righty Ray Narleski finished at 3-3 in 42 appearances, but both had a slew of key saves during the campaign.

The hitters did their job as well. Larry Doby regained the AL home run lead, with 32, and also led the circuit in RBIs, with 126. Second baseman Bobby Avila was the batting champ at .341, and third sacker Al Rosen hit .300 while also supplying the Tribe with added power. Outfielder Al Smith hit a solid .281, while first baseman Vic Wertz, a midseason acquisition, batted .275 with good power.

In the National League the Giants came on to replace the Dodgers as senior circuit kingpins. While Brooklyn got its usual array of fine performances from its hitters, the pitching faltered, and that gave the Giants the invitation they wanted. They had plenty of wherewithal to make the most of the opportunity, beginning with the great Mays. Back from the army, the Say Hey Kid simply tore up the league. He was the top hitter, with a .345 mark, smacked 41 home runs and collected 110 RBIs. In addition, he ran the bases like a demon and played centerfield better than anyone. He was an easy choice as Most Valuable Player. And he wasn't the Giants' only asset.

Outfielder Don Mueller hit .342, with a league-leading 212 hits, while Al Dark batted .293. Others, like Whitey Lockman and Monte Irvin, didn't have as good numbers as in the past, but Mays managed to raise the level of everyone's game, and he had help from an unlikely source.

His name was James Lamar Rhodes, though everyone called him "Dusty," and he would spend seven seasons with the Giants between 1952 and 1959. He was never more than a utility player, mainly a pinch hitter, because asking him to play in the field was like asking a mouse to walk through a field of cats. Lifetime stats show that Rhodes was really no more than a mediocre hitter. His average for his years in the Bigs was a modest .253. But for one year, in 1954, Dusty Rhodes became Superman. In just 164 at bats that year, Rhodes had 15 homers, 50 RBIs and a .341 average. Even more important was the fact that whenever the Giants needed a key hit that year Dusty Rhodes seemed to get it. The bigger the game, the more likely that Rhodes would deliver. And he knew it. Whenever there was a chance for the Giants to turn a game around, Rhodes would approach manager Leo Durocher and, in his Alabama drawl, say, "Ah'm your man, Skip."

The pitchers did their jobs, too, beginning with a 21-7 record from lefty Johnny Antonelli,

**Opposite left and above:** This sequence shows Mays making one of the greatest catches in World Series history. The grab came in game one of the 1954 Series. The hitter was Vic Wertz of the Indians.

**Opposite below:** Big Ted Kluszewski of the Reds crosses home plate after belting another home run. The Red's first baseman led the NL, with 49 round-trippers in 1954.

acquired in a trade with the Braves for 1951 hero Bobby Thomson. Sal Maglie had a 14-6 log, while Ruben Gomez finished at 17-9 and Don Liddle at 9-4, and the one-two bullpen tandem of Hoyt Wilhelm and Marv Grissom was enough to take the Giants over the top.

In addition to the surprise pennant winners, there were a number of other outstanding individual hitting performances during 1954. On 2 May Stan The Man Musial lived up to his nickname once more when he blasted a record five home runs in a doubleheader against the Giants. And later in the year big Joe Adcock, the Milwaukee first baseman, tied a mark by hitting four consecutive homers in a game against the Dodgers. Adcock had a double in his only other at bat, enabling him to establish still another standard, that of 18 total bases in a single game. And Cincy first baseman Ted Kluszewski, a National Leaguer since late 1947, had his greatest year, with 49 homers and 141 RBIs, topping the circuit in both departments.

Despite all these National League accomplishments and the success of the Giants, it was the Cleveland Indians who were overwhelming favorites when the World Series began. And why not? The team had won 111 games during the regular season, and they had all that pitching.

The Series opened at the old Polo Grounds in New York, Bob Lemon taking the hill for the Indians against veteran Sal Maglie of the Giants. When the Indians jumped on Maglie for two first-inning runs it looked as if they were off and running. But the Giants tied it in the third, and it stayed 2-2 all the way into the bottom of the tenth inning. The reason it remained 2-2 was because of an incredible catch made by Willie Mays in the eighth inning.

Cleveland had put two runners on and had Vic Wertz coming up to the plate. Wertz was red hot, with four hits already, and he promptly tagged one off lefty Don Liddle. The ball rocketed toward deep center, where the old clubhouse sat some 483 feet from home plate. Mays took off at the crack of the bat and raced toward the clubhouse, not even looking at the flight of the ball. Still running full speed and about 440 feet from home plate, Willie suddenly reached up and caught the ball over his left shoulder, his back still turned toward home plate. It's considered by many the greatest catch in World Series history. Without hesitating, he then turned and fired the ball back to the infield, keeping the runners from advancing.

In the tenth inning, with the score still knotted at 2-2, Mays walked with one out, stole second and stayed there as Henry Thompson was walked intentionally. Then up stepped James

Lamar Rhodes. Dusty parked one just over the wall down the right field line for a three-run pinch hit homer that defeated Lemon and won the game for the Giants.

That set the stage for an improbable Giants' sweep. Rhodes also figured heavily in game two. The Giants were trailing 1-0 in the fifth, when the pinch-hitter supreme singled in the tying run and set up the go-ahead score that paved the way for a 3-1 New York victory behind Johnny Antonelli. In game three the Giants had a 1-0 lead and the bases loaded in the third inning. Going to his bench very early, Durocher sent up Rhodes, and

**Below:** Dusty Rhodes, a magical pinch hitter for the 1954 Giants, carried his big bat right into the World Series.

**Right:** Don Larsen of the Yankees was little more than a journeyman pitcher until he threw a perfect game in the 1956 Series.

once again Dusty singled, driving home two and leading the Giants to a 6-2 victory. Rhodes wasn't even needed the next day when the New Yorkers wrapped up the Series with a 7-4 victory, Dark and Mueller having three hits each.

For the Series, Rhodes had four hits in six trips and drove home a team-leading seven runs. "Ah'm your man, Skip."

One sad note. Because of the Giants' sweep, Bob Feller didn't get in a single game. So Rapid Robert was again denied in his quest to win in the World Series. He wouldn't get another chance.

The 1955 season was the one in which "next year" finally came. After getting into the World Series six times and coming out on the losing end on all six occasions, the Brooklyn Dodgers made their long-suffering fans believers. They climaxed another great year by defeating the mighty Yankees in seven games. But like most everything else in baseball, it didn't come easy.

As the season began the geographical face of the game continued to change. First it had been the Braves, moving from Boston to Milwaukee. Then the St Louis Browns became the Baltimore Orioles. And before 1955 there was still another move. This time it was that ancient franchise, the Philadelphia Athletics. The team was sold, and the new owners promptly moved the ballclub to Kansas City, Missouri, as the Kansas City As. (The franchise would subsequently move to Oakland, California, and a new team, the Kansas City Royals, would be created.)

Even the mighty Yankees faced some problems as the new season began. While the Bombers still had the firepower to bust down fences, the pitching staff had become a question mark. Raschi and Reynolds were gone, and Lopat was fading fast. So much for the big three. Trying to rebuild around Whitey Ford and the 1954 rookie sensation, Bob Grim, the Yanks swung a massive trade with the Orioles, giving up several young pitchers, a good catching prospect named Gus Triandos and a great veteran in Gene Woodling. In return the New Yorkers got a slew of utility players and a number of pitchers, the two keys being righthanders Don Larsen and Bob Turley. Neither could win with the hapless Orioles (Larsen was an appalling 3-21 in 1954, and Turley was 14-15), but the Yanks figured the two could turn it around in New York. It was also the rookie year for catcher-outfielder Elston Howard, the Yankees' first black player. Howard would hit a solid .290 in 97 games and go on to a fine career with the Bombers.

With Stengel once again pushing the buttons, the Yanks found themselves in the midst of another pennant race. Cleveland was there again, and in the early going so was Chicago and Boston. The four teams were neck-in-neck. For a time the Indians had the lead, and it looked as if they would repeat. Boston dropped back, but the White Sox hung tough, as did the Yanks. Finally the Yankees wrapped it up with a sizzling finish that saw them take off on a 15-game winning streak. That clinched it. They won it by three over the Indians and five over the Sox.

Mickey Mantle emerged as the new American League home run champion, with 37, and the Switcher also hit .306 and drove home 99 runs. Teammate Berra, while hitting just .272, had 27 circuit clouts and 108 RBIs and won the Most Valuable Player award for the third time, the last two in a row. And there was the usual support from the likes of Hank Bauer, Phil Rizzuto, Joe Collins, Billy Martin, Gil McDougald, rookie Howard and Irv Noren.

Ford topped the pitchers, with an 18-7 mark, while lefthander Tommy Byrne had his best year, at 16-5. Turley was 17-13 in his first Yankee season, while Larsen finished 9-2. Another youngster, Johnny Kucks, helped out at 8-7, while Bob Grim, Rookie of the Year in 1954, slipped to 7-5. But it was enough to win.

So with the Yanks winning, some things stayed the same. But they were changing in other ways. Young Al Kaline of the Tigers became one of the youngest batting champions in baseball history by compiling a .340 mark at the age of 20. Ray Boone of the Tigers and Jackie Jensen, now with the Red Sox, tied for the RBI lead with 116 each. And while the American League didn't have a

**Above:** Elston Howard was the first black man to don a Yankee uniform when he joined the Bombers in 1955.

**Left:** Mickey Mantle was swinging a big bat during the 1956 season when he won the American League triple crown. The Mick had 52 homers, a .353 batting average and 130 RBIs.

single 20-game winner, the junior circuit nevertheless had itself a mound phenom. His name was Herb Score, and as a 22-year-old rookie with the Indians the flamethrowing lefthander compiled a 16-10 record and had a major league best of 245 strikeouts. With the great Bob Feller's career almost at an end, Score suddenly seemed the logical successor as baseball's fastest pitcher and premier strikeout artist. He was an easy choice as American League Rookie of the Year for 1955.

In the National, the Dodgers really didn't have any trouble regaining their pennant-winning ways. They established superiority immediately, winning 22 of their first 24 games, and by the end of April they were leading the league by a whopping 9½ lengths. The Brooks kept up their frenetic pace and actually clinched the pennant on 8 September, the earliest winning date in National League annals. They ended up with a 98-55 record, finishing 13½ games ahead of second-place Milwaukee and 18½ ahead of the fading Giants, whose manager, Leo Durocher, resigned at the end of the season.

Brooklyn got its usual array of fine performances under skipper Walter Alston. Jackie Robinson, at age 36, had slipped noticeably in 1955, hitting just .256 in 105 games. But the others were as good as ever. Catcher Campanella duplicated Yogi Berra's feat by winning his third Most Valuable Player prize. Campy batted .318, hit 32 homers and drove home 107 runs. Gil Hodges hit a solid .289, while Furillo had a .314 average. Reese was still solid at .282, and then there was the Duke.

Edwin Donald Snider had been with the Dodgers since 1947, and in the mid-fifties he had

become such a good ballplayer that he was ranked up there with both Mays and Mantle. That not only gave the New York teams three of the best centerfielders in baseball, it also helped precipitate a never-ending argument among New York baseball fans. Who was the best, Willie, Mickey or the Duke?

Snider was coming off a pair of seasons in which he hit .336 and .341. And he did it with power. In 1955 he still weighed in with a solid .309 and 42 homers and led the National League in RBIs, with 136. Edwin Snider was one fine ballplayer, a man well worthy of his nickname.

Dodger pitching was also strong that year. Newcombe re-emerged as the ace of the staff, with a 20-5 record. Erskine had dropped off to 11-8, but Billy Loes checked in at 10-4 and Clem Labine had his best year at 13-5. Rookies Don

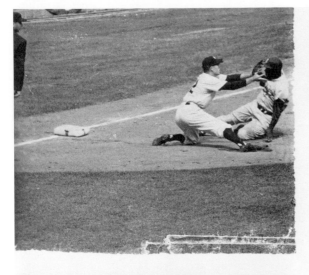

**Left:** In the twilight of his career, Dodger Jackie Robinson still got around the bases. Here he slides into third with a triple in the first game of the 1955 World Series.

**Below:** "Moose" Skowron was part of the Yanks' home run club in the 1950s.

Bessent and Roger Craig also contributed a combined 13-4 record down the stretch. But young lefty Johnny Podres was something of a disappointment at 9-10. Still, the Dodgers felt they would be ready for the Yanks.

It was a big year for power hitters in the National League. Willie Mays led the circuit with 51 home runs, while hitting .319. Big Ted Kluszewski belted 47, Ernie Banks 44 and Eddie Mathews 41. And the youngster, Henry Aaron, in just his second full season hit .314, with 27 round trippers and 106 RBIs. The batting champion was the Phils' Richie Ashburn, at .338.

There was another player of note who made his National League debut in 1955. Roberto Clemente, a native of Puerto Rico, joined the Pittsburgh Pirates at the age of 20. Clemente batted a modest .255 in 124 games that year, but before his untimely death in a plane crash while bringing aid to Nicaraguan earthquake victims in 1972, Clemente would win four batting titles and collect 3000 basehits. He was one of the finest all-round players of his generation.

The World Series of 1955 opened at Yankee Stadium, and, because of their previous track record, the Bombers had to be the favorites. When they won the first game 6-5, KOing Newcombe and getting two homers from Joe Collins

Left: Lefthander Johnny Podres was the hero of the 1955 World Series when he won the 7th game with a 2-0 shutout of the Yanks, giving the Dodgers their first World Series win ever.

Below: Roy Campanella set to embrace Podres after his historic win.

and one from Elston Howard, the Yanks seemed to be on their way. Whitey Ford was the winner, with help from Bob Grim.

Game two was again all Yanks. This time the Bombers broke loose against Billy Loes for four runs in the fourth inning, and Tommy Byrne yielded only five hits in a 4-2 Yankee victory. Not only did the Yanks have a 2-0 lead in games, they had done it without Mickey Mantle, who was nursing another of his numerous leg injuries. But he was due back for the third game, so how could the Yanks lose?

Yet returning to the friendly confines of Ebbets Field was like a tonic for the Dodgers. Manager Alston started Johnny Podres in game three, and the young lefty went the distance, defeating the Yanks 8-3. Mantle returned to homer for the Bombers, but Roy Campanella had three hits, a homer, and three ribbys for the Brooks.

Carl Erskine started game four for the Dodgers against Bob Turley, and the Yanks got him out early, taking a 3-1 lead in the top of the third. But then the Dodgers dragged out the big guns. Campanella, Snider and Hodges all homered, as the Brooks rapped out 14 hits and tied the Series with an 8-5 victory. And when Snider whacked two more homers in game five, leading the Dodgers to a 5-3 win behind young Roger Craig, Brooklyn had come all the way back to take a 3-2 lead in games. Everyone wondered if the long-suffering Flatbush fans would finally have a World Series champion?

But now the scene switched back to Yankee Stadium, the House that Ruth Built, and the Yanks had their ace, Whitey Ford, ready to go. Alston surprised everyone by gambling on young lefty Karl Spooner. The gamble failed. Spooner didn't get out of the first inning, as the Bombers scored five times, the highlight being a three-run homer by first baseman "Moose" Skowron. And Ford made it hold up, throwing a four-hitter for a 5-1 Series-tying victory.

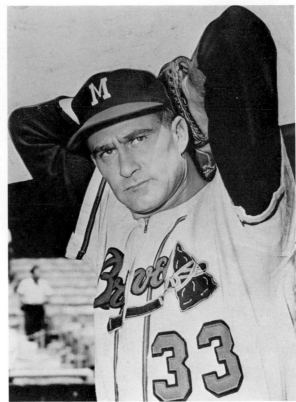

**Above left:** Yankee Manager Casey Stengel congratulates Dodger skipper Walt Alston after 1955 Series.

**Above right:** Lew Burdette of the Braves was a mound mainstay in the late 1950s.

The deciding game had the veteran Byrne against the youngster Podres in a battle of lefties. And it *was* a battle. The Dodgers managed just five hits but pushed across a run in the fourth and another in the sixth. Meanwhile, Podres was using a fine changeup to go with his fastball in scattering eight hits. Sandy Amoros saved the day by making a great catch of a Yogi Berra drive in the fourth, and Podres did the rest, completing a shutout and giving the Brooklyn Dodgers the first world championship in their history.

A quick postscript to the Dodgers' first title. Brooklyn had a young lefthander on the team that year. He appeared in just 12 games and had a 2-2 record in 42 innings. His name was Sandy Koufax. Though he threw very hard, his control was spotty and his pitching mechanics poor. The team wasn't sure what the future held for him, and they didn't trust him enough to allow him to pitch in the Series. But the first step up a mountain is sometimes a very small one.

There were no more franchise shifts at the beginning of the 1956 season, but there were rumblings. Most of the rumors centered on the fact that the world champion Dodgers had scheduled seven games at Roosevelt Stadium in Jersey City, New Jersey, instead of at Ebbets Field. It was inconceivable that the Dodgers would be contemplating a shift to nearby New Jersey. The stadium there was minor league, but many felt that the rescheduling was the prelude to some kind of move. Dodger owner Walter O'Malley simply would not reveal his plans. The whole thing seemed even more strange since the Dodgers were one of the two most successful

teams in the game over the past decade. Ebbets Field wasn't large, but the fans were faithful. And the Brooks were favorites to repeat as National League champions in 1956.

That, they did, but not without sharp challenges by both the Milwaukee Braves, a team that had been coming on for several years, and the Cincinnati Reds, a surprise ballclub that began busting down fences all over the league. The three clubs would battle down to the wire, with the race not decided until the final days of the season.

The Braves had great balance – between pitching and hitting, between youth and age, between speed and power. The great Warren Spahn was joined by fidgety Lew Burdette and steady Bob Buhl to form a big three on the mound. Young Henry Aaron continued to come into his own as a great player, and he joined Ed Mathews and Joe Adcock as long-ball threats. The team was also strong up the middle, with catcher Del Crandall, shortstop Johnny Logan and speedy centerfielder Billy Bruton.

Cincinnati developed a nearly overpowering team in 1956. The Redlegs would tie the record set by the 1947 Giants by blasting 221 home runs, led by Ted Kluszewski and Wally Post, both of whom had over 40 homers. Outfielder Gus Bell and catcher Ed Bailey could also pop the ball out. But the biggest lift came from a muscular rookie named Frank Robinson.

Robinson was a 20-year-old rookie from Beaumont, Texas, who would not only be the Rookie of the Year in the National League, but would go on to become a Hall of Fame player,

author of 586 lifetime home runs, the first player to win the Most Valuable Player Award in both leagues and eventually the first black manager in big league history. But that was to come. All Frank Robinson did in 1956 was bat a solid .290 in 152 games and blast a rookie-record-tying 38 home runs to contribute mightily to the Cincinnati cause. And, ironically, the first season of a great player named Robinson was also the last season of another great player who was likewise named Robinson.

At age 37 Jackie Robinson would still hit a respectable .275 for the Dodgers, with 10 homers and 43 RBIs in just 117 games. But the great pioneer was only a shell of his former self. When he learned he had been traded to the rival Giants following the 1956 season, Robby made his decision. "My legs were gone and I knew it," he said. "It would have been unfair to [Giants' owner] Horace Stoneham and the Giants to take their money." So Jackie would retire with a .311 lifetime batting mark in just 10 seasons. But his skills, competitiveness and great courage were enough to earn him an eventual place in Baseball's Hall of Fame. To get there, he paid a special price.

The three-way National League pennant race was decided when the Dodgers eliminated Cincinnati and then squeaked in ahead of the

**Above:** In 1955 Dodgers and their fans swarm onto the field when Brooklyn wins its first World Series.

**Left:** Frank Robinson of the Reds burst onto the baseball scene in 1956 with a rookie record-tying 38 homers.

Braves. Brooklyn's margin of victory over Milwaukee was a single game, and they bested Cincy by just two. This time the Dodgers were led by big Don Newcombe, who put together an absolutely superb season, finishing with a 27-7 record, good enough to earn him the Most Valuable Player prize, as well as the newly-

created Cy Young Award for the best pitcher in baseball.

And Newcombe had help. Although Campanella slumped to .219, Duke Snider led the league in homers, with 43, and hit .292. Carl Furillo had another good year at .289. Some of the others had off years, but the team was still good enough to milk another pennant out of their aging lineup. Young Aaron, incidentally, won his first batting title, at .328, while Stan Musial topped the senior circuit in ribbys, with 109. Big Newk was joined by Warren Spahn and Johnny Antonelli as 20-game winners.

In the junior circuit the Yanks found the going much easier. The Bombers had their usual powerful team and in 1956 got an extra added ingredient. Mickey Mantle finally reached the great potential everyone had predicted for him from day one. The Mick started the year by blasting a pair of opening-day homers over the centerfield fence in Washington, and before he was through he would win the triple crown, the first player to do it since Ted Williams, nine years earlier.

Mantle, in fact, had 47 homers going into September, and there was talk that he would better Babe Ruth's mark of 60. Perhaps it was the pressure, perhaps just a routine slump, but Mickey tailed off a bit in the power department and finished with 52 round-trippers. Add to that a .353 batting average and 130 runs batted in and you've got a super season, the one everyone had been expecting for so long.

The Yanks had to fight off a challenge from the speedy Chicago White Sox, a team that featured players like Nellie Fox, Minnie Minoso, Jim Rivera and a rookie shortstop named Luis Aparicio who, beginning in 1956, would lead the American League in stolen bases for nine consecutive years. The Pale Hose also had some power with newly-acquired Larry Doby and catcher Sherm Lollar. But the Sox didn't have the pitching, and they faded after the All-Star break. Cleveland, as usual, had the pitching but not the hitting, so the Yanks won it by nine over the Indians, 12 over the Sox.

For Cleveland young Herb Score continued to look like the superstar pitcher of the future. In his

**Above:** Yankee ace Whitey Ford at work during the 1956 World Series against the Dodgers. Always a money pitcher, Ford would later hurl more than 30 straight scoreless innings in World Series play.

**Left:** Yogi Berra gets a welcoming committee after belting a grand slam in the second game of the '56 World Series, which was won by the Yanks in seven games.

**Opposite:** During his triple crown season of 1956 Mickey Mantle was as powerful a hitter as ever played the game.

second season the fireballing lefthander compiled a 20-9 record and once again led the league in strikeouts, with 265 whiffs. Score was joined by teammates Bob Lemon and Early Wynn as 20-game winners, while Frank Lary and Billy Hoeft of Detroit, as well as Billy Pierce of Chicago, also reached the charmed circle.

One other pitching note. Cleveland's great righthander, Bob Feller, called it quits following the 1956 season. Rapid Robert compiled a career mark of 266-162, with 2581 strikeouts , a record that would have been much better had he not lost four prime seasons to the military. Had his career gone uninterrupted, Feller surely would have won well over 300 ballgames and fanned more than 3000 hitters. No wonder he's in the Hall of Fame.

The World Series in 1956 featured the two MVPs, Mantle and Don Newcombe. Each would figure in the outcome of the fall classic, but the show would be stolen by another hurler who would pitch the kind of game many thought impossible in the World Series.

Ebbets Field was the site of game one, and the Dodgers surprised everyone by tabbing 39-year-old Sal Maglie as their starting pitcher. Sal the Barber, as he was called, had had his greatest years with the rival New York Giants. He had gone to Cleveland the year before, then came to the Dodgers early in the 1956 season. Regaining his old curve ball and some old magic, Maglie

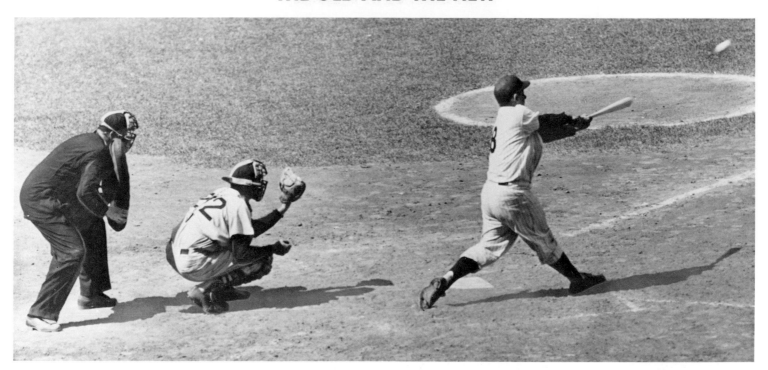

backed up Newcombe with a 13-5 record. Now he was starting game one of the Series.

The Yanks, of course, went with Whitey Ford, who was 19-6 during the regular season. And when the Bombers got a pair of runs off Maglie in the first inning it looked as if manager Alston had made a mistake. But the veteran settled down, and the Dodgers got to Ford for two in the second and three more in the third, as Hodges and Robinson belted home runs. Brooklyn took the opener by a 6-3 margin.

Game two was a slugfest. Newcombe started against Don Larsen, and the game was tied at 6-6 after two innings, with both starting pitchers out. The Dodgers got the better of the relief work and went on to a 13-8 triumph, giving them a commanding 2-0 lead in games as the Series returned to Yankee Stadium for the third contest.

Now the Bombers came back. They won that one 5-3 behind Ford, then took game four, winning 6-2 behind knuckleballer Tom Sturdivant, to pull even at two games each. Next came the pivotal fifth game. Manager Alston sent Maglie to the mound once more, and Stengel decided to counter with Don Larsen, who had been roughed up so badly in game two.

A big righthander, Larsen was 11-5 during the season and had come on after switching to a unique no-windup delivery, which he felt would keep him from tipping his pitches. Early on, the game had all the earmarks of a pitcher's battle. Both hurlers were perfect for three innings. Then, with two out, in the fourth, Mantle picked out a Maglie offering and blasted it into the seats for a home run and a 1-0 Yankee lead. The Yanks got a second run in the sixth, Hank Bauer driving it home. Larsen, however, had still given up nothing.

Now the tension was building. Both Yankee and Dodger fans remembered Bill Bevens' bid for a no-hitter in the 1947 Series, when Cookie Lavagetto broke it up with a game-winning double in the ninth. But now Larsen was working on a perfect game, which seemed even more inconceivable in World Series play than a no-hitter. Yet the big guy kept retiring Dodgers, one-two-three, one-two-three, one-two-three.

Finally he was just three outs away. All 64,519 fans at Yankee Stadium were on the edge of their seats, as were the players on both teams. Could Larsen do it? He had benefited from a running backhanded catch by Mantle in left center on a drive by Gil Hodges. But otherwise he had been absolutely brilliant.

Carl Furillo was the first batter in the ninth, and he lofted an easy fly for the first out. Next came Campanella. The ever-dangerous Campy grounded weakly to Billy Martin at second. Now there were two out, and lefty swinger Dale Mitchell was coming up to hit for Maglie, who had also pitched a beautiful ballgame.

Mitchell took Larsen's first pitch for a ball, then the second for a strike. He went after the third, but missed it. Strike two. The next one was fouled off. So Larsen had to do it again. Still pitching without a windup, he fired a fastball. Mitchell checked his swing, but umpire Babe Pinelli's right hand went up in the air. Strike three!

Larsen had done it, the first perfect game and no-hitter in World Series history. Catcher Berra ran to the mound and leaped into Larsen's arms, and the rest of the Yanks followed suit. It had been an amazing performance, and it gave the Yanks a 3-2 lead in the Series.

Not only had Larsen's performance made

**Opposite top:** The scoreboard tells the story as the Yanks' Don Larsen hurls the only perfect game in Series history against the Dodgers in 1956.

**Opposite bottom:** Catcher Yogi Berra bearhugs Larsen after the final out of the 2-0 gem.

**Above:** Always a deadly clutch hitter, Yogi Berra was at his best when the chips were down. He was a three-time AL MVP.

**Above:** Pittsburgh's Ralph Kiner and the Cards' Red Schoendienst both had fine careers. Here they share a happy moment as the co-heroes of the 1950 All-Star Game.

baseball history, it also put the Dodgers' backs against the wall. Returning to Ebbets Field, the Dodgers sent one-time reliever Clem Labine to the mound to face the Yanks' Bob Turley who, like Larsen, used the no-windup delivery. This one was also a classic, going ten innings. It was still a scoreless tie when the Dodgers came to bat in their half of the tenth. They had just three hits off Turley, but a walk, a sacrifice and an intentional walk put runners on first and second, with one out and Jackie Robinson up. Robby had already stranded five runners in the game, but this time the great veteran came through, slamming a line drive over Enos Slaughter's head in left to drive home the winning run. It would be the last hurrah of Jackie's career.

So the Series was tied again, but a day later it all came apart for the Dodgers. Newcombe was on the mound again, this time facing young Johnny Kucks, who had won 18 games during the year but had never pitched in this kind of pressure cooker before. Many felt that big Newk was overdue for a strong game and that the Dodgers would win. But in baseball anything can happen. The Yanks had four runs off Newcombe by the third inning, all scoring on a pair of two-run homers by Berra. The Bombers got one more in

the fourth and four more off reliever Roger Craig in the seventh, to win the game and regain their championship 9-0, as young Kucks pitched a three-hit shutout.

While the 1956 Series will always be remembered for Larsen's perfect game, it is also significant for other reasons. The abject failure of Don Newcombe to pitch well forever stigmatized the big righthander as a pitcher who failed in the clutch, when in truth Newcombe was always an outstanding mound performer. It was also the final major league appearance of Jackie Robinson, baseball's greatest pioneer and one of its most courageous performers.

And perhaps even more significantly, the 1956 World Series marked the end of an era in which the Brooklyn Dodgers dominated the National League. The Dodgers would return to the fall classic in another three years, but by then the face of the team would have changed significantly. There would not only be new players, but a new location, one that would be some 3000 miles away from Ebbets Field and Flatbush and Bedford Avenues, so long associated with the Brooklyn Dodgers.

The 1957 season was really a prime example of the old and the new. For starters, the players now

had a union. The Major League Baseball Players' Association had officially begun on 1 October 1956. The union would play a large role in players' salaries and pensions in the years to come.

Also, shortly after the season started it became obvious that the Dodgers were not going to repeat. Age was catching up with many of the star players. Robinson was gone, and he was always a catalyst. The Milwaukee Braves, second by just a game in 1956, saw the opportunity to break through.

Milwaukee had a solid core of pitching and hitting stars, and just before the halfway point in the season really solidified the team by acquiring veteran second baseman Al "Red" Schoendienst from the Giants. Schoendienst had been a star with the Cardinals since 1945, and, at age 34, he was coming off a .300 season in 1956 and had hit .307 in 57 games with the Giants prior to the trade. Joining Aaron, Mathews, Adcock, Logan, Crandall and the rest, he gave the team some more savvy and put glue in the infield.

The Dodgers were out of it early. St Louis hung tough into the second half, but it was soon apparent that the Braves would win it. And while they were in the process, they were also setting a new major league attendance record.

Milwaukee had a brace of fine performances in 1957, but perhaps the best came from Henry Aaron. Now taking his place besides Mantle and Mays, Aaron led the National League, with 44 home runs and 132 runs batted in. He hit a solid .322 but didn't win the triple crown because 36-year-old Stan Musial took his seventh batting title, with a .351 average. The Man added 29 home runs and 102 RBIs. He could still get the job done.

Aaron had plenty of hitting support, and the Braves also got fine pitching. Warren Spahn (21-11) was a 20-game winner for the eighth time in his career. Bob Buhl was 18-7, and Lew Burdette 17-9. The Braves were a worthy successor to the Dodgers as National League champs. And the common denominator would be their opponents, for once again the New York Yankees were the class of the American League.

The Bombers started the year with the same formidable cast of characters, including a young infielder named Tony Kubek, who would hit .297 and be Rookie of the Year. The Cleveland Indians, with their strong pitching, were expected to challenge again. When the two ball-clubs met in early May, it was considered a key early series. But it turned into a series that produced one of the most tragic accidents in baseball history.

**Above left:** Like most great players, the Braves' Hank Aaron kept getting better and better. When his team won the National League pennant in 1957, Hammerin' Hank was the league's Most Valuable Player.

**Above:** Shortstop Tony Kubek was typical of the fine caliber of ballplaying by the New York Yankees in the 1950s and early 1960s. The steady Kubek was a .266 lifetime hitter.

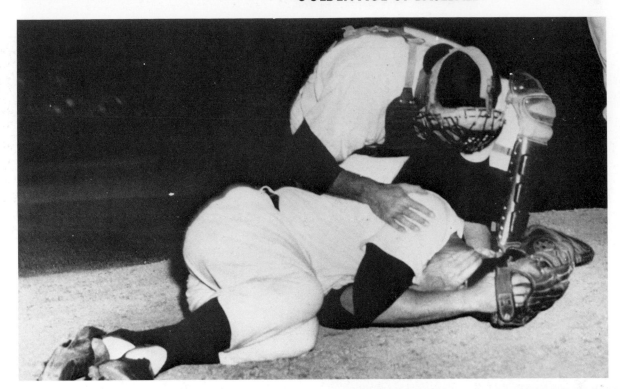

**Left:** Catcher Jim Hegan comforts Cleveland pitcher Herb Score seconds after Score was hit by a line drive off the bat of the Yanks' Gil McDougald in May of 1957.

**Opposite top:** A typical packed house at the old Polo Grounds in New York as the host Giants meet the Dodgers in 1952.

On 7 May the Indians started their ace, Herb Score, against the Bombers. Score was 2-1 in four starts in the early going, but everyone expected another big year for him. Score was facing infielder Gil McDougald in the very first inning when it happened. McDougald went after one of Score's blazers and slammed a hard line drive right back at the box. Score tried to get his glove up, but couldn't, and the ball caromed off his right eye. The pitcher went down in a heap, and ballplayers from both teams rushed out to the mound.

The injury was a severe one. Score was having vision problems and was finished for the season. A disconsolate McDougald threatened to quit baseball, though doctors said Score would recover. But when the lefty returned the next year something wasn't right. Whether he was gunshy, or whether his vision still wasn't perfect, or whether he had just changed his delivery, no one seemed to know. But he wasn't the same pitcher, and never would be. He hung around the majors for another five years, but the best he could do was 9-11 in 1959. Then he retired to become a broadcaster in 1962 at the age of 29. In just a split second a line drive had altered a career that seemed destined for greatness.

Soon the Yanks were comfortably ahead of the rest of the field, and Mickey Mantle was having another fine year. His homers and RBIs were down somewhat, but his batting average was up, and that seemed to augur another batting title. The only fly in the ointment was named Ted Williams.

Williams was hitting over .300, as usual, in the first half of the season. But he was 39, and no one thought the Splendid Splinter would be able to

catch Mantle. In fact, most thought he would tail off during the hot weather of July and August. Instead, Ted caught fire, hitting an incredible .453 during the second half of the season. On two separate occasions he belted three home runs in a single game. Late in the year he passed Mantle and kept going.

Mantle would finish the 1957 season with a career high .365 mark. His 34 homers and 94 RBIs were good enough to earn him a second straight Most Valuable Player prize. But many thought that honor should have gone to

**Above:** Ted Williams of the Red Sox accepting a plaque from the Sporting News as the Player of the Year for 1957. All the 39-year-old Williams did that year was win the AL batting title with a .388 average. Presenting the award are Ollie Rodman (l) and Bob Holbrook.

Williams, for the Splinter wound up leading the league with an amazing .388 average. Age at 39 he had come within five hits of a second .400 season. In just 420 at bats Ted had 38 home runs and 87 ribbys, an unforgettable performance by one of the great hitters in baseball history.

There were other fine performances, too. Roy Sievers of Washington was the new homer and RBI champ in the AL, with 42 and 114 respectively. Jim Bunning of Detroit and Billy Pierce of the White Sox were the league's only 20-game winners, but the Yanks, with their depth and balance, were easy pennant winners.

Before the races were decided and the World Series could get underway, baseball was rocked with some news that would really alter the structure of the game. By now people had gotten used to franchise shifts. The moves of the Boston Braves, St Louis Browns and Philadelphia As were old news, mainly exciting for the cities involved. In any case, all the big league teams were still located east of the Mississippi River. But when Horace Stoneham of the New York Giants called a news conference in mid-August, the announcement he made shocked everyone. He told the baseball world that the Giants, a National League mainstay in New York since 1883, would open the 1958 season in San Francisco, California! The team had drawn only some 629,000

fans to the outmoded Polo Grounds in 1956, and things weren't getting any better, despite the presence of a great player like Willie Mays. So the Giants would be moving west.

Baseball people suspected something more was in the wind. They didn't think Horace

**Above:** Jim Bunning of the Tigers had a 20-8 record in 1957 and would win more than 100 games in both leagues.

Stoneham would have acted alone, and he hadn't. In the midst of the World Series the Dodgers' Walter O'Malley announced that his team would be leaving Brooklyn for the glitz and glamour of Los Angeles, California. So the beloved Bums, in Brooklyn since 1890, would also be decamping. O'Malley didn't have attendance problems, but Ebbets Field was small and old, and O'Malley saw the prospect of unlimited riches on the West Coast. As it turned out, he was right.

So as the 1957 World Series was played the prospect of coast-to-coast baseball was just around the corner. And both the Polo Grounds and Ebbets Field would eventually be razed for apartment complexes, the beginning of an era that would see many of the older ballparks abandoned and eventually torn down.

The news of the Giants and Dodgers moving to the West Coast was enough to steal any show, and the World Series might have been anti-climactic that year, had it not been for one of the great individual performances in Series history. The action started in New York, and when Whitey Ford whipped Warren Spahn in the opener 3-1, it looked like business as usual for the Yanks. Then, in game two, the Braves turned to Burdette, who had been Yankee property at one time. The nervous righthander had all kinds of fidgety moves on the mound, moves many construed as an attempt to cover up a tendency for Lew to "load up," in other words, throw an illegal spitball.

New York went with little Bobby Shantz, who had gone 11-5 after coming over from Kansas City. Both clubs exchanged single runs in the

**Above:** The Braves' Lew Burdette en route to one of his three wins in the 1957 Series against Yanks.

**Left:** Hank Aaron slams a home run in the fourth game of the 1957 Series.

second and third innings. Then the Braves got two in the fourth, to bounce Shantz and take a 4-2 lead. That was all Burdette needed. He throttled the Yankee bats and completed a 4-2 victory.

Back in Milwaukee the Yanks showed the Braves' loyal fans some old fashioned Bronx Bomber brawn. They erupted for 12 runs, including a pair of homers by rookie Kubek and one by Mantle, as they cruised to a 12-3 win and a 2-1 lead in the Series.

With a chance to go up by two in game four, the Yanks couldn't do it. Homers by Aaron and Frank Torre helped the Braves to a 4-1 lead into the ninth. But a three-run homer by Elston Howard off Spahn tied the game. When the Yanks got one in the 10th, it looked over, but the Braves got one back in their half of the inning, and then Eddie Mathews hit a two-run shot to win the game 7-5.

Now it was Burdette's turn again. This time he locked horns with Whitey Ford in what turned into a classic. Big Joe Adcock drove in the only run of the game, as Burdette threw a seven-hitter and won it 1-0. Back at Yankee Stadium the Bombers drew even, Turley on the winning end

of a 3-2 victory. Now came the decisive game. Warren Spahn was slated to go for the Braves against Tom Sturdivant of the Yanks. But the great lefty came down with the flu and couldn't pitch. Manager Fred Haney had no choice but to turn to Burdette, who would be pitching with just two days rest.

But the veteran righthander was more than equal to the task. Once again mixing a fastball with tantalizing off-speed pitches, he baffled the Bombers for a third time, spinning another seven-hitter as the Braves won 5-0, bringing a world championship to Milwaukee, a city that hadn't even had a major league team until five years earlier. It was a storybook ending.

As for Burdette, he had pitched three complete games, two of them shutouts, and had given up just two runs in 27 inning, and none in the final 24. His tremendous performance fell only a shade short of duplicating the immortal Christy Mathewson's three complete-game shutouts in the 1905 World Series.

As 1958 approached, two of the games' oldest franchises were packing their bags. Many traditionalists opposed the move, but no one could deny the game was growing.

**Below:** New York fans follow their team to the clubhouse after the Giants' last game at the Polo Grounds (1957).

# CHAPTER VII
# BASEBALL COAST TO COAST

Seals Stadium, the temporary home of the San Francisco Giants.

California wasn't really ready for major league baseball. While there was a great deal of anticipation among the fans, there were no spanking new ballparks awaiting the Dodgers and Giants. Willie Mays & company would be playing in the minor league Seals Stadium, while the Dodgers would be forced to use a football and track stadium, the huge Los Angeles Coliseum, the layout of which for baseball was totally unsatisfactory, with a ridiculously close leftfield fence 251 feet from home plate, while the rightfield fence sat a distant 440 feet away.

But Walter O'Malley was more than ready to put up with the 102,000 seating capacity until he could build his own ballpark. Before the team arrived for the 1958 season, however, there was a terrible tragedy. As a result, LA fans would never get to see one of the greatest of Dodgers in action.

In the early morning hours of 28 January, Roy Campanella was driving home from the liquor store he owned in New York City when his car skidded on the wet road, hit a telephone pole and overturned. Campy was pinned in the car, seriously injured. When he was finally taken to a hospital the news was bad. He had broken his neck and was paralyzed from the chest down. Though he recovered from his injuries, he would spend the rest of his life in a wheelchair, never again to display his great skills on the diamond. But the three-time MVP had been good enough in 10 short years to eventually be named to baseball's Hall of Fame.

The first major league game ever played on the West Coast took place on 18 April when the Giants visited the Dodgers at the Coliseum. Walter O'Malley must have felt vindicated immediately when some 78,000 fans showed up. It would have taken more than two full houses at Ebbets Field to rack up that kind of number.

Unfortunately, the LA fans would not see the Dodgers as the faithful of Brooklyn had known them. Many of the veteran players made the move to LA, but they were now on the far side of 30 and past their prime. Snider and Furillo had good years, but Pee Wee Reese was a part-timer in his final campaign. Newcombe was traded shortly after the season began, Robinson and Campanella were gone and Carl Erskine was a shell of his former self. The club had a promising righthander named Don Drysdale, who won 17 games in 1957 but would be just 12-13 in '58. And that enigmatic lefthander, Sandy Koufax, still hadn't found consistency, though he was 11-11 in the first year in LA. With all these problems, the team finished seventh, just two games out of the basement.

The Giants did a bit better. They were third and gave the fans of the Bay area a look at some

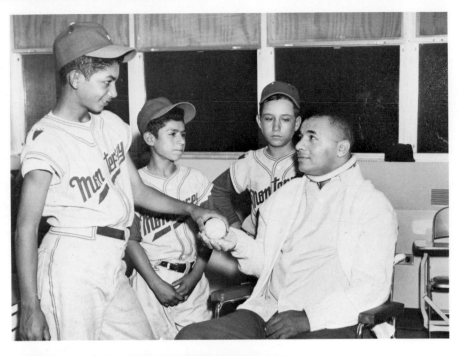

great individual talent. Mays hit a career-best .347 and added 29 homers and 97 RBIs, along with 31 stolen bases and his usual sensational play in center field. To many he was still the best all-round player in the game, but he would never attain the kind of popularity or total appreciation that he had had in New York. It was as if the fans on the Coast never quite accepted him as one of their own.

One reason might have been Orlando Cepeda, a big Puerto Rican-born slugger who was a Giants' rookie in 1958. Cepeda hit .312 in his first year and belted some long home runs. He was a unanimous choice as Rookie of the Year, and he quickly became a fan favorite, someone who had started his career in California and didn't have the New York roots.

**Above:** Injured catcher Roy Campanella talks with Mexican Little Leaguers.

**Left:** Giants' slugger Orlando Cepeda was Rookie of the Year in 1958.

**Opposite top:** Before his injury Roy Campanella (39) was one of baseball's top sluggers.

**Opposite bottom:** This is the first Dodgers game at the LA Coliseum.

While baseball was getting started on the Coast, the Milwaukee Braves were efficiently putting together another pennant-winning season, finishing an easy eight games ahead of Pittsburgh. Spahn won 22 and Burdette 20, while Aaron and company took care of the hitting, Hammerin' Hank leading the way with a .326 mark.

Richie Ashburn of the Phils won his second batting championship, at .350, while Ernie Banks, Mr Cub, belted 47 homers, a record for a shortstop, and drove in 129 runs to lead the league in both categories. Banks would also be voted the league's Most Valuable Player, despite the fact that his team finished sixth.

The American League race was getting to be old hat. It was the Yankees again, their fourth straight AL pennant and their ninth in ten years under Casey Stengel. The Bombers finished with a 92-62 record, not great, but no one really challenged them. Chicago wound up second, ten games behind, giving the New Yorkers a comfortable margin of victory.

Though his average dropped to a modest .304, Mickey Mantle regained the AL home run lead, with 42, and also drove home 97 runs. Catcher Berra had 22 home runs and 90 ribbys, while Whitey Ford was 14-7 on the hill, with seven shutouts and a 2.01 earned run average. But the guy who really helped the 1958 Yanks retain their title was Bullet Bob Turley. The fireballing righthander, in his fourth season with the Yanks, put together a Cy Young Award-winning season with a 21-7 record and was the team's stopper all year.

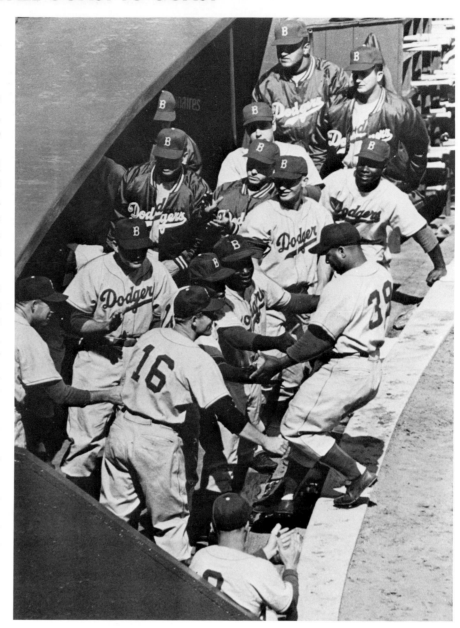

**Top:** The great Ted Williams won his sixth and final batting title in 1958 with a .328 average.

**Above:** A smiling Ernie Banks has just learned he is the National League's Most Valuable Player for 1958. The Cubs' shortstop belted 47 home runs.

The batting champion in 1958 shouldn't have surprised anyone. By now, people should have known that Ted Williams was just about capable of anything with a Louisville Slugger in his hands. At age 40 the Splendid Splinter took his sixth AL bat crown with a .328 average, out-hitting teammate Pete Runnels by six points. It would be Williams' final batting title, but there probably would hae been even more had he not lost five peak seasons to military service.

Jackie Jensen of Boston was the RBI king, with 122, and also the league MVP, while a little out-fielder with the Washington Senators, Albie Pearson, was the Rookie of the Year. With the exception of Turley, there were no other 20-game winners in what was a rather uneventful year. The only remaining question was whether the Yanks would regain the championship from the Braves. That wouldn't be easy.

It was a battle of lefties in the opener at Milwaukee's County Stadium, as Whitney Ford squared off against Warren Spahn. Despite home runs by the Bombers' Hank Bauer and Moose Skowron, the game was tied at 3-3 after nine, and in the tenth Bill Bruton of the Braves singled home the winning run off reliever Ryne Duren. Down one game, the Yanks now had to face Lew Burdette, who had beaten them three times in the Series of 1957.

Fidgety Lew had thrown two shutouts and recorded 24 consecutive scoreless innings against the Bombers in that one, but now, in the top of the first, the Yanks broke through for a run against the righthander. Had they broken the Burdette jinx? That hope lasted only a few minutes. For in the bottom of the first inning Milwaukee scored seven big runs off Bob Turley en route to a 13-5 victory. Burdette had a three-hitter going into the ninth, but then Bauer and

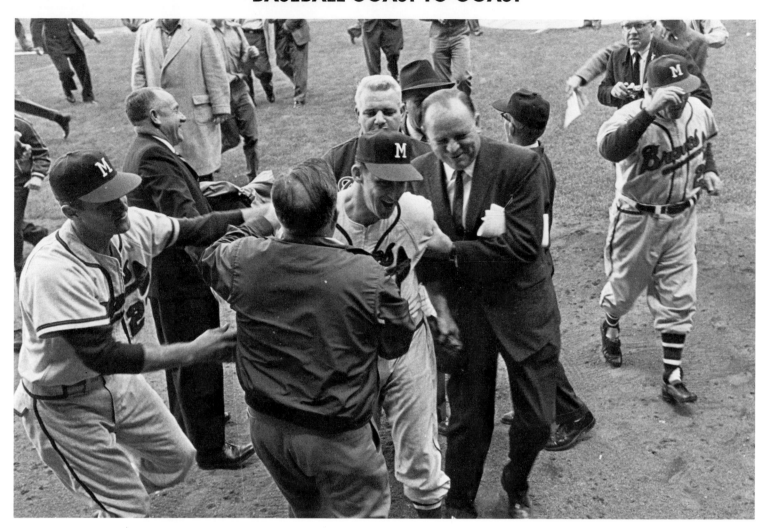

Mantle homered, the Mick's second homer of the game. Yet even though the New Yorkers had gotten to Burdette, they had lost big and were suddenly in bad trouble at two games to nothing.

Returning to Yankee Stadium, Don Larsen and Ryne Duren combined for a six-hit shutout to give the Yanks a 4-0 victory. But when Warren Spahn pitched a brilliant two-hitter in game four, besting Whitey Ford 3-0, the Yanks trailed 3-1 in games. Only the 1925 Pittsburgh Pirates had rallied from a 3-1 deficit to take the Series.

It was Bob Turley who took up the challenge in game five, shutting out the Braves on five hits. The game had to be especially satisfying because the Yanks finally KOed Lew Burdette, getting six runs in the sixth inning en route to a 7-0 victory. Back in Milwaukee for game six, the Yanks got two in the top of the tenth, then held off a Milwaukee rally for a 4-3 victory over Warren Spahn. Now it was tied and down to a single game.

Don Larsen got the call for the Yanks, while Lew Burdette was once again tabbed as the Milwaukee starter. They were the same two pitchers who squared off in the seventh game a year earlier. Larsen didn't have it, and by the third inning Turley had come on, but the Yanks had a 2-1 lead. Milwaukee tied it in the sixth, as the two pitchers continued to throw well. But then in the

eighth inning the Yanks broke it open, scoring four times, three of them coming home on a Moose Skowron home run. It ended at 6-2, and the Yanks had done it, becoming the second team ever to rally from a 3-1 deficit. They were champs again, and they had lived up to their nickname of Bombers, with 10 homers, four of them by Hank Bauer.

While 1958 was relatively devoid of memorable individual performances, the next year more than made up for it. For starters, there were surprise pennant winners in both leagues, with an exciting three-way race in the National. The Braves pretty much had their entire team back. They were already two-time winners and had missed by just a game the year before that. So they were odd-on favorites once again.

The challenge came from the West Coast, where suddenly both the Dodgers and Giants had become bona fide contenders. San Francisco had been third in 1958, an 80-74 team that still had Willie Mays, the rookie Cepeda and some other sound players. So their challenge wasn't really a shock. But the Dodgers were a different story. LA had all but bombed out in their first year on the Coast. The Campanella tragedy had had a demoralizing affect on the team. In addition, many of the players who had carried the team for so long were now on the

**Above:** Milwaukee's great lefthander, Warren Spahn, is congratulated after he shut out the Yankees 3-0 in the fourth game of the 1958 World Series. The 37-year-old southpaw won 22 games during the 1958 regular season and in spite of his advancing age would have four more 20-win seasons before he retired at the age of 44 in 1965.

downslide. The result was a 71-83 seventh place finish. But the team was bringing some younger players into the fold and in 1959 they began to put it together sooner than anyone expected.

The club still had some of the mainstays from the 1940s and 1950s. Duke Snider continued to be a productive player in center, while Gil Hodges and his moments at first. Jim Gilliam had moved over to third, and Johnny Podres, the World Series hero of 1955, had become a mainstay, though he was not now a superstar. Clem Labine continued to anchor the bullpen. But now all these veterans had help.

Young John Roseboro was the new catcher. He didn't have the consummate skills of a Campanella but was a solid backstop. Second baseman Charley Neal could hit with some power, and by the end of the season the shortstop was a 27-year-old rookie named Maury Wills, who added base-stealing speed to the lineup. Outfielders Wally Moon, Don Demeter and Norm Larker all made major contributions, as did another young first baseman-outfielder named Ron Fairly. Pitchers Stan Williams and Larry Sherry gave help to the vets, and somehow manager Walter Alston pasted it all together.

But before the pennant race could really heat up, something occurred that had the whole baseball world buzzing. On 26 May the Pittsburgh Pirates were at Country Stadium in Milwaukee for a night game against the Braves. Milwaukee started one of its aces, Lew Burdette, while the Pirates countered with a little lefty, Harvey Haddix. Haddix was a cutey who reminded people of that old Cardinal, Harry "The Cat" Brecheen.

As a result, Haddix was nicknamed "The Kitten," and he was indeed a pretty crafty pitcher. He had been a 20-game winner back in 1953 and had won 18 the following year, but he also had had seasons of 12-16 and 10-13. Traded to the Pirates in 1959, Haddix was en route to a mediocre 12-12 season. And when he took the mound against Burdette and the powerful Braves that night, no one imagined he was about to make baseball history.

**Above:** Pittsburgh's Harvey Haddix pitched perhaps baseball's greatest game in 1959 when he threw 12 perfect innings against the Braves.

**Right:** LA Dodger manager Walter Alston shares smiles with pitcher Roger Craig (l) and outfielder Don Demeter after the club ties for 1st on September 23, 1959.

**Opposite top:** Yankee pitcher Bob Turley (19) jumps for joy after the final out of the 1958 World Series. The Bombers beat the Braves in seven games.

**Opposite below:** Dodger out-fielders Wally Moon (l) and Duke Snider collide on a fly ball hit by White Sox Sherm Lollar in game one of the 1959 Series.

The game began uneventfully enough, but before long the story started flickering out across the teletypes to all the other parks in the league. And pretty soon the wire services began picking up on it too. Haddix was pitching a shutout. In fact, he was pitching a no-hitter. But even better than that, he was pitching a perfect game! Not a single Brave had reached first base.

No one paid that much attention in the early innings, but when the game went past the fifth,

then the sixth and into the seventh, all eyes began to turn to Milwaukee. Haddix was still perfect, but there was another element to the game as well. The Pirates still had not scored on Burdette. Though they were getting almost a hit an inning, sometimes two, Burdette would always work out of trouble. A scary thought began crossing baseball minds. What if Haddix remained perfect but his team couldn't get him a run?

That's just what happened. At the end of nine

innings the game remained a scoreless tie. And Harvey Haddix had retired all 27 Milwaukee Braves he had faced. Yet he couldn't celebrate what should have been one of pitching's greatest gems. No, he had to trudge back out to the mound in the 10th inning to face the Braves once more. And now everyone was watching and waiting.

Once again Harvey Hadix retired the Braves in one-two-three fashion. He did it again in the eleventh and then the twelfth. But at the same time, Lew Berdette kept working out of jams, refusing to allow the Pirates a run. Haddix had set down 36 Braves in order, the greatest pitching performance the game had ever seen. And he still hadn't won.

In the top of the 13th the Pirates again failed to score, and Haddix had to come out again. How long could it go on? The answer came quickly. Felix Mantilla led off for the Braves and hit bouncer to Don Hoak at third. It looked routine until Hoak threw the ball away! The perfect string had been broken. Ed Mathews was next, and he bunted Mantilla over to second. Haddix then walked the dangerous Hank Aaron intentionally, bringing up slugger Joe Adcock. The big guy caught one, driving a Haddix offering over the fence in right center for an apparent game-winning three-run homer. It was over, all right, but Aaron, figuring Mantilla's run had ended it, touched second and headed for the dugout. So when Adcock circled the bases, he was technically ruled out for passing Aaron. His hit went in the books as a double.

Nevertheless, it made Harvey Haddix a 1-0 loser in 13 innings, even though he had been perfect for 12. Burdette, by contrast, had given up 12 singles, yet he had prevented the Pirates from scoring. It's hard to think of a stranger game.

M eanwhile, the pennant race continued, all three NL teams battling into the second half. During the final third of the season the Giants brought up a big 21-year-old first baseman from the minors. His name was Willie McCovey, later to be known as "Stretch." McCovey would hit .354, with 13 homers, in 52 games, to give the Giants the Rookie of the Year for the second consecutive season. He teamed with Mays, Cepeda and outfielder Willie Kirkland to supply power to the pennant push. Though it would take McCovey a few more years to really establish himself, he would eventually go on to a long career that would result in 521 home runs and a trip to the Hall of Fame.

But the Giants didn't have the pitching to stay with the Dodgers and Braves for the entire year. By September it became apparent that it would be either Milwaukee, winning its third straight pennant, or the Dodgers, rising from the seventh

**Above:** Pittsburgh's Don Hoak gets safely back to first before the Giants' Willie McCovey can put a pick-off tag on him. This action took place in May of 1960.

**Opposite top:** The Braves' Ed Mathews, shown here as a 20-year-old rookie in 1952, became one of baseball's top sluggers for over a decade and finished with 512 homers.

**Opposite bottom:** White Sox skipper Al Lopez pats veteran hurler Early Wynn on the shoulder before he removes him from the sixth game of the 1959 World Series. Wynn won 300 games during his long career.

place of the year before. And when the season ended the two teams were deadlocked with identical 86-68 records, forcing a best-of-three playoff. To the surprise of nearly everyone the Dodgers took the Braves in two straight, winning the first game 3-2 at Milwaukee, then the second 6-5 in 12 innings at Los Angeles, rallying in both the ninth and twelfth innings to wipe out Braves' leads. So the Dodgers would be in the World Series once again, only this time representing the City of Angels.

LA had won the crown with a collective effort from the entire team: the outstanding individual performances were supplied on other teams. Henry Aaron of the Braves had one of his finer seasons, winning the National League batting title with a career-best .355 average. He also added 39 home runs and 123 RBIs, reaffirming that he was one of the greats. The home run crown went to Aaron's teammate, Eddie Mathews, who had 46, while the Cubs Ernie Banks, with 143 runs batted in, not only led the majors in that category, but became the first player ever to win the Most Valuable Player prize two years in a row. Warren Spahn, at age 38, won 21 games, the 10th time in his career he was over 20; and that number was equalled by teammate Burdette and by Sam Jones of the Giants.

In the American League there were also a few surprises. For one thing, it became obvious early on that the Yankees were not going to make it five in a row. The Bombers, for some reason, just couldn't get going, and they also had a number of key injuries. Whenever the Yanks weren't in the chase, which hadn't been too often since the later 1940s, there was heightened interest in the AL pennant race. And in 1959 it was between those perennial runners-up, the White Sox and Indians.

The Pale Hose were spearheaded, oddly enough, by several ex-Indians, notably manager Al Lopez, veteran pitcher Early Wynn and outfielder Al Smith. The club also had a great keystone combination in shortstop Luis Aparicio and second baseman Nellie Fox. Veteran power hitter Ted Kluszewski had come over from Cincinnati, while Jim Landis and Jim Rivera gave the club speed in the outfield. And Sherm Lollar was a good veteran catcher.

Wynn, who would win 22 games and the Cy Young Award at age 39, had good mound support from righthanders Bob Shaw, Dick Donovan and Gerry Staley, as well as from veteran lefthander Billy Pierce. They all helped break open a close race at the end of August by whipping the Indians in four straight, allowing the Sox

SCREEN 40 FT.

PORTABLE FENCE

250 FT.

TEMPORARY BOX SEATS

RIGHT FOUL LINE 300 FT.

HOME PLATE

*West*

to eventually capture the flag by five full games. So the Pale Hose would be the first American League team to travel to the West Coast when they met the Dodgers in the World Series.

Besides the great season put together by Wynn, there were a number of other fine White Sox performances. Nellie Fox, who played in every game and hit .306, was the league's MVP. Aparicio really stole the show with 56 thefts on the year, while pitcher Shaw was 18-6.

Other AL stalwarts included Detroit's Harvey Kuenn, who won the batting title with a .353 mark, and Boston's Jackie Jensen, who repeated as the RBI leader with 112. Bob Allison, who hit .261 with power, gave Washington the Rookie of the Year for the second straight time. The home run crown was shared in 1959 between Cleveland's Rocky Colovito and Washingtons Harmon Killebrew. Both had 42. Killebrew had first appeared with the Senators in 1954 when he was just 18 years old. But he didn't win a regular job until 1959. Then, playing in 153 games, he showed his awsome power potential by tying Colovito for the home run title. And it wasn't a fluke. A powerful righthanded batter who never hit for a great average, Killebrew would play for 22 seasons and clout 573 home runs, good enough for fifth place on the all-time list.

The World Series opened in Chicago, though most of the anticipation centered on the LA Coliseum, with its strange configuration and its potential for enormous crowds. But that was all forgotten once the White Sox went to work in the first game. The Pale Hose made it look easy. They got two in the first, then KOed starter Roger Craig with a seven-run outburst in the third, highlighted by a Kluszewski home run. Big Klu hit another in the fourth, as the Sox cruised to an 11-0 victory. Early Wynn went seven strong innings before his elbow stiffened, and veteran Gerry Staley completed the shutout.

The Dodgers started Johnny Podres in game two, and the Sox countered with Bob Shaw. When the White Sox got a pair off Podres in the first it looked as if they were off and running again. But then the lefty put the brakes on the Sox attack, and the Dodgers finally scored a run when Charley Neal homered off Shaw in the fifth. Then, in the sixth, Chuck Essegian batted for Podres and smacked a homer to tie the game. After Shaw walked Gilliam, Neal promptly clouted his second circuit of the game, giving the Dodgers a 4-2 lead.

With Larry Sherry pitching for the Dodgers, the Sox rallied in the eighth, the big hit being an Al Smith double with two runners on. The first

**Above:** This was how officials planned to alter the Los Angeles Coliseum for baseball in 1958. The huge football stadium was used by the Dodgers when they first moved west.

**Opposite:** A youthful Harmon Killebrew in 1959 was ready to emerge as one of baseball's most feared sluggers.

scored, but the second, Sherm Lollar, was nailed at the plate on a perfect relay from outfielder Wally Moon to shortstop Willis to catcher Roseboro. It saved the game and iced a 4-3 Dodger victory, paving the way for the Series to move to Los Angeles.

As expected, a huge crowd, 92,394 fans, surged into the cavernous Coliseum to see the first-ever World Series game on the West Coast. They wouldn't be disappointed. With big Don Drysdale on the mound, the Dodgers took a 3-1 victory, giving them a 2-1 lead in the Series. Chicago outhit LA 12-5, but Drysdale and reliever Sherry had what was needed when it counted. Now it would be Wynn and Craig again in game four.

For the second time in two days a crowd in excess of 92,000 filled the Coliseum. This time Wynn didn't have it. The Dodgers knocked the veteran righthander out with a four-run outburst in the third inning. Craig held the Sox scoreless until the seventh. Then Chicago rallied, scoring one run before Sherm Lollar belted a three-run homer to tie the game. That brought Larry Sherry into the Series for the third time. Finally, in the bottom of the eighth, veteran Gil Hodges came up against reliever Staley. Turning the clock back to Ebbets Field days, the 35-year-old veteran belted the home run that gave Sherry and the Dodgers the win, 5-4, and a commanding 3-1 advantage in games.

Trying to clinch the Series before still another crowd of 92,000 plus, the Dodgers gambled on their erratic lefty, Sandy Koufax, while the Sox countered with Bob Shaw. Koufax had been with the team since 1955, and while possessed with

incredible raw talent, he still hadn't been able to put it together. He often overthrew his fastball and had trouble controlling his curve. The result had been a modest 8-6 record in 1959, though he had fanned 173 hitters in 153 innings. And in a game against the Giants on 31 August, Koufax had tied a major league record by striking out 18 batters. So while he was a risk in the Series, the potential for an outstanding game was there.

Sure enough, the 6' 2", 198-pound lefty pitched exceedingly well, striking out six, while walking just one, in seven innings. He gave up only five hits and a run in the fourth, which came across on a pair of singles and a double-play grounder. Unfortunately for Koufax and the Dodgers, Bob Shaw was equal to the task, shutting out the Dodgers for 7 1/3 innings before Bill Pierce and Dick Donovan came on to finish the job. The 1-0 finale kept the White Sox alive and sent the Series back to Chicago for a sixth game.

Johnny Podres, as he had been four years earlier, was given the chance to pitch his team to

**Above:** Pee Wee Reese, then a coach, and Don Drysdale (53) help celebrate the Dodgers' 1959 World Series victory.

**Left:** Ace Dodger reliever Larry Sherry won two and saved two in the '59 Series.

the championship. The Sox once again turned to their best, the aging Early Wynn. Unfortunately, the great veteran was out of gas. The Dodgers got to him for a pair in the third, then sent him to the showers with six big runs in the fourth. They now had a seemingly insurmountable 8-0 lead. But of course they didn't dare to relax when facing a team like the Sox. When Podres faltered in the bottom of the inning, as the Sox scored three times, manager Alston went back to Larry Sherry, who once again shut the Sox down, allowing the Dodgers to coast to a 9-3 victory and a World Series triumph for Los Angeles.

Ted Kluszewski was the big man for the Sox, hitting three homers and driving home 10 runs in six games. But the real hero of the series was reliever Sherry, never more than a journeyman pitcher, who had appeared in four of the games, winning two and compiling a 0.71 earned run average. He was the Series MVP, proving once again that you never can predict heroes and goats in the game of baseball.

Baseball was now entering a new decade, and there were already plans afoot that would alter the basic structure of the sport for years to come. Perhaps the seeds were sown by the rousing success of the Dodgers and Giants on the West Coast. Why had baseball been so slow to see that there were other cities that would welcome a major league team? The franchise shifts of recent years had all worked out very well. So there were some who felt that the moves to Los Angeles and San Francisco were only the beginning of a larger migration.

In 1959 it had suddenly been announced that a group of investors were planning to start a third major league. It was to be called the Continental League and would have as its president none other than Branch Rickey, the man who had broken baseball's color line by signing Jackie Robinson. Since putting a new league into operation would be a very difficult task, those behind the Continental League sought the help of Congress, asking to have some of the laws governing

**Above:** Candlestick Park in San Francisco as it looked a month before the Giants began playing there for the first time in 1960. Today the park is completely closed in to keep the winds out.

baseball changed. When this approached failed, plans for the Continental League were gradually abandoned.

But the possibility of a rival league spurred the majors to action, and before the 1960 baseball season would end, it would be announced that the big leagues would be expanding for the first time since the American League was formed in 1901. For 59 years there had been eight teams in each league. Now the number would be increased to ten. Plans called for new National League franchises in New York and Houston, beginning in 1962. The American League moved even faster. The 1961 season would see the Washington Senators become the Minnesota Twins, while a new franchise (also to be called the Senators) would be formed in Washington, and a second new franchise would be brought into Los Angeles.

So it was an exciting time for the game, but before expansion could be implemented the 1960 season had to be completed. And it would prove an interesting season in a number of ways. For one thing, it looked like the end of one of baseball's great careers was at hand.

After winning successive batting titles in 1957 and 1958, the latter coming at the age of 40, Ted Williams had found the going tough in 1959. He hurt his neck during the offseason and never really got on track. Playing in just 103 games the Splendid Splinter had had the first sub-.300 season of his life. He batted just .254, with 10

**Above:** Ted Williams getting his last hit as a Red Sox. In that 1960 season he hit .316, with 29 homers.

**Opposite top left:** Veteran baseball innovator Branch Rickey tried to start a third major league in 1959, but the venture failed.

**Opposite top right:** Second baseman Bobby Richardson was another fine Yankee star in the late 1950s and 1960s.

**Opposite bottom:** The great Brooks Robinson of the Orioles is called by some the best third baseman ever.

homers and 43 RBIs. To most observers, including Red Sox owner Tom Yawkey, Ted seemed finished and Yawkey suggested to the Splinter that he call it quits.

But Ted Williams wasn't about to go out on such a low note. The competitive fires still burned, and Williams said he would take a $35,000 pay cut just to play another year. So he suited up once more, and at the age of 41 he was going out there to show people that the old man could still hit.

The other big question in the American League was whether the Yankees could rebound from the 79-75 season of 1959. Never a team to stand pat, the Bombers always seemed to get new players when they needed them. By 1960 they were slowly putting a new infield in place, with Bobby Richardson taking over at second and Clete Boyer moving in at third to join with shortstop Tony Kubek. But perhaps their biggest acquisition in 1960 came in a trade with Kansas City. His name was Roger Maris, a 25-year-old outfielder who had started his career with Cleveland in 1957. Maris had shown flashes of power but had never played a full season at either Cleveland or KC. He would take over in right for the Yanks and prove to be quite a find.

In fact, Casey Stengel had a very powerful Yankee team in 1960, nothing like the year before. The Bombers cruised to the American League pennant, winning by eight games over the surprising Baltimore Orioles, who got some

heavy hitting from first baseman Jim Gentile and catcher Gus Triandos, as well as from a 23-year-old third baseman named Brooks Robinson.

Robinson had first come up to the Birds when he was barely 18 in 1955. But by 1960 he had finally become an everyday player, and during the course of a career that would last through 1977 he would become the finest fielding third baseman of his era, or perhaps any era, as well as a leader and clutch hitter. In fact, Brooks Robinson was so good that he was elected to the Hall of Fame in 1983.

And speaking of the Hall of Fame, one of its future occupants was now busy proving his point. Taking up the challenge after being told he was finished, Ted Williams showed once again why he is considered by many the greatest hitter the game has ever known. Determined to go out on a high note, the Splendid Splinter got his way. Playing in 113 games, a number of them as a pinch hitter, the now 42-year-old Williams batted .316 in 310 at bats. Better yet, he crashed 29 homers and managed to drive in 72 runs.

Early in the season he had cracked his 500th home run, and by season's end he had 521 for his career. Without those years lost to the service, Williams would have surely hit somewhere around 650 circuits for his career. Better yet was Ted's farewell game at Fenway park in late September. Coming to the plate against Baltimore lefty Steve Barber in what would be his last big league at bat, the Splinter spanked one. He hit a

hard line drive into the right centerfield bullpen for a home run. And as he circled the bases for the last time, taking his .344 lifetime average, all those home runs and all the thrills of a great career with him, he had to be satisfied that he had proven his critics wrong. He had gone out with a bang, not a whimper, and that's the only way he'd have it.

As to other American League developments in 1960, Mickey Mantle regained the home run lead with 40, though his batting average slipped to .275. The league MVP? It was Mantle's new teammate, Roger Maris. In his first Yankee season Maris hit .283, clubbed 39 home runs and drove in a league-leading 112 runs. In addition, Maris proved to be one of the better defensive outfielders in the league. The batting champ was Pete Runnels of Boston, at .320, while shortstop Ron Hansen of Baltimore was the Rookie of the

Year. But surprisingly, there wasn't a single 20-game winner in the entire league.

In the National League it was expected to be more of the same, which meant either the Dodgers or the Braves. Both teams had basically the same cast of characters, though many experts favored the Braves because of the nucleus of Spahn, Burdette, Aaron and Mathews. What nobody expected was a big challenge by the Pittsburgh Pirates.

The Bucs hadn't won a pennant since 1927, and that year they were the unlucky team to face the Murderer's Row Yankees of Babe Ruth and Lou Gehrig. Naturally they lost in four straight games. After that it was mostly famine, including a brace of last place finishes in the late 1940s and early 50s, despite the presence of superslugger Ralph Kiner. The team continued to struggle, finishing last in 1954, 1955 and again in 1957.

But in 1958 the Bucs suddenly had jumped to second behind Milwaukee, compiling a surprising 84-70 record. They settled back to fourth the following year, with a 78-76 mark, in spite of a fantastic 18-1 record compiled by reliever Elroy Face. So the Pirates weren't considered serious contenders when the first year of the new decade rolled around. But under manager Danny Murtaugh the Bucs had corraled a number of fine ballplayers.

The leader of the team was shortstop Dick Groat, a player who got the most out of his talent. Groat had been an all-American basketball star at Duke University but had opted for baseball. A solid player for a decade, Groat would put together his greatest season in 1960, just when the Bucs needed it the most.

If Groat was the leader, Roberto Clemente was also a star. Now entering his sixth full season with the Pirates, the Puerto Rico-born outfielder

**Opposite:** Ted Williams had vowed never to doff his hat to fans. He broke the vow only once, before his last game as a big league player on September 26, 1960.

**Above:** Dick Groat was a basketball all-American at Duke before becoming a star shortstop with the Pirates and National League MVP in 1960.

**Top:** Pirates' Manager Danny Murtaugh (l) and reliever Roy Face arrive at Forbes Field before the seventh and final game of the 1960 World Series.

was just maturing as a hitter and complete ballplayer. While Groat would hit .325 in 1960, Clemente would be right behind, at .314. The club had some other good sticks as well, such as outfielders Bill Virdon and Bob Skinner, first baseman Dick Stuart (called Dr. Strangeglove for his work in the field), catcher Smokey Burgess and second sacker Bill Mazeroski.

But it was when the Bucs developed a solid pitching staff that the team really become tough. Righthander Vernon Law was a 20-game winner and the ace of the staff. Big Bob Friend, solid as always, won 18. Harvey Haddix and Vinegar Bend Mizzell were proven veterans, and Elroy Face was perhaps the best reliever in baseball.

It was a cast of characters who managed to put it all together for a single season. The Bucs surprised everyone with a 95-59 record, good enough for the National League pennant and a seven-game bulge over second-place Milwaukee. (A year later, with things not falling into place nearly as well, the Bucs once again became a sub -.500 team, at 75-79.)

Groat was voted the league's Most Valuable player and also took the batting title for the only time in his career. Ernie Banks took his third homer crown, with 41, while Hank Aaron welcomed in the new decade by driving home 126 runs, best in the league. Dodger shortstop Maury Wills ended Willie Mays' four-year run as the league's stolen base champ when he swiped 50 sacks. Slugger Frank Howard of the Dodgers was Rookie of the Year, while Spahn and the Cubs' Ernie Broglio joined Law as 20-game winners.

Big Don Drysdale of the Dodgers led the league with 246 strikeouts, but more interest now began centering on his teammate, Sandy Koufax. The hard-throwing lefthander had an 8-13 record in 1960, giving him just a 36-40 mark for six seasons in the league, but there were some who persisted in seeing greatness in this pitcher who couldn't seem to get his amazing "stuff" under control. In 175 innings he fanned 197 hitters. The year before he had struck out 173 in 153 innings. Yet he also walked 100 batters in 1960, even though giving up only 133 hits.

Koufax was frustrated. It's said that he once had words with Dodger general manager Buzzie Bavasi, in which he demanded to pitch more. When he asked how he could be expected to get anyone out when he didn't pitch, Bavasi supposedly answered: "Get the ball over when you do pitch. You've got one pitch – high."

The Giants were visiting the Coliseum the night of that exchange and Willie Mays overheard it. The Say Hey Kid later told an LA writer, who was also on the scene, "I wish they'd get mad enough to trade him to us." Willie certainly called that one right.

But Koufax would have to wait another year to get his wish. In the meantime, the Yankees and Pirates prepared to square off in one of the strangest World Series of all time. Just look at the basic numbers.

In seven games the Yankees batted .338. They scored 55 runs and collected 91 hits, 27 of them for extra bases. Ten of their hits were home runs. Second baseman Bobby Richardson, normally a singles hitter, drove in six runs in a single game, belted a grand slam homer and totalled 12 RBIs for the Series. Moose Skowron had 12 hits, two homers and six RBIs, while Mantle smacked out 10 hits, clubbed three homers and drove home 11. As a team, the Bombers set a slew of World Series hitting records. They won games by lopsided scores of 16-3, 10-0 and 12-0, both shutouts authored by Whitey Ford.

The Pirates, on the other hand, scored just 27 runs, made just 60 hits and four home runs. But they won games by scores of 6-4, 3-2 and 5-2. So believe it or not, this very unusual World Series came down to a seventh game, which was played at old Forbes Field on 13 October 1960. Vernon Law and Bob Turley were the starters, but before this one ended a total of nine pitchers would trudge out to the mound.

This time it was the Bucs who started quickly. Rocky Nelson slammed a two-run homer in the first, and Bill Virdon drove in another pair with a single in the second. Suddenly the Pirates had a 4-0 lead, with their ace on the mound. It stayed that way until the fifth, when Moose Skowron homered for the first Yankee run. Then, in the sixth inning, Law ran out of gas.

When Richardson singled and Tony Kubek walked, manager Murtaugh replaced Law with Elroy Face. But the little righty was pitching in his fourth Series game and was tired. Mantle promptly smacked a single, to drive in one, and then the clutch-hitting Yogi Berra belted a

three-run homer. The Yankee thunder had struck, and the Bombers had the lead, at 5-4. But the fun was just beginning.

In the top of the eighth the Yanks moved to get some insurance runs. Face was still pitching when a walk to Berra, followed by singles off the bats of Skowron and Johnny Blanchard, plus a double by Clete Boyer, gave the Bombers two runs and a 7-4 advantage. They were now just six outs away from another World Series triumph.

But Pittsburgh simply wouldn't quit. In the bottom of the eighth, pinch hitter Gino Cimoli singled off Bobby Shantz. Bill Virdon was next, and he hit what looked like a doubleplay bouncer at shortstop Kubek. But at the last second the ball took a freak hop and struck Kubek right in the throat. Both runners were safe, and Kubek had to leave the game. That opened the doors.

Groat singled home one run, and Jim Coates took over for Shantz. A sacrifice by Skinner moved the tying runs into scoring position, but they were forced to hold when Nelson skied to right for the second out. Then Clemente got an infield hit, as Virdon scored, bringing the Bucs within one, at 7-6. Next came reserve catcher Hal Smith. All he did was belt a three-run homer to complete a five-run rally and give the Pirates a 9-7 lead. Now Pittsburgh was three outs away from a championship, and the veteran Bob Friend came in to try to close it out.

He couldn't. The Yanks got a pair of baserunners, and Mickey Mantle singled one home. Berra then drove home the second tally on a hard grounder to first baseman Nelson. Now the game was knotted at nine, as Pittsburgh prepared to hit in the bottom of the ninth. Manager Stengel then made another move, bringing righthander Ralph Terry in to face leadoff hitter Bill Mazeroski.

Maz wasted no time. He took Terry's first pitch for a ball, then slammed the second one over the leftfield wall for a World Scrics-winning home run. It was a shot that rivaled Bobby Thomson's immortal 1951 blast, and the city of Pittsburgh went wild. Their Pirates had won the World Series, an improbable end to the first year of the new decade.

**Above:** A jubilant Bill Mazeroski crosses home plate after the ninth-inning homer that won the 1960 Series for the Bucs.

**Opposite top:** The awesome Mickey Mantle returns to the dugout after belting another World Series homer in 1960.

**Opposite bottom:** Bob Friend saw both the good and the bad in Pittsburgh, winning 22 games in 1958, but losing 19 the following year.

# CHAPTER VIII
# EXPANSION

Big league expansion had been much on the minds of most baseball fans when the 1960 season ended. The American League was about to add two new teams and increase the schedule from the longstanding 154 games to 162. With the Washington franchise moving to Minneapolis-St Paul, there would be a new team in Washington, also called the Senators, as well as a new ballclub in Los Angeles, to be known as the Angels. And plans were also being made to add two new National League franchises the following year.

But somehow the big expansion story constantly found itself pushed onto the back burner in 1961. It seemed that whenever someone turned to the sports pages during the year there was another surprising new story to read. It started five days after the end of the World Series.

That's when the baseball world learned that Casey Stengel had been unceremoniously fired from his post as the manager of the Yankees. It was hard to believe. Ol' Case had managed the Yanks for 12 years and in that time had won 10 pennants and seven World Series. That was about as close to perfect as any manager could get. In addition, Stengel had led the Bombers to the last four AL flags in a row. It was hard to believe that he would get the ax just because the Yanks had lost in seven wild and crazy games in 1960. The official line was that Case, at 70, was too old to continue at the helm. To which the old man answered in typical Stengel fashion, "I'll never make the mistake of being 70 years old again."

The housecleaning continued with the dismissal of general manager George Weiss, the architect of the great Yankee teams of the 1950s. There may have been no rationale for the moves, but at least the new manager proved to be a popular figure. He was Ralph Houk, a one-time third-string catcher for the Bombers who later became a coach. Nicknamed "The Major" for his days in the rugged Rangers unit in World War II, Houk would always be a players' manager who wouldn't hesitate to be in the thick of any kind of trouble on the field.

That was only the beginning of the new season's surprises. Dodger lefthander Sandy Koufax had not been having a good spring. Once again his fastball was wild and unpredictable, and he had begun to feel he'd never put it together. As he rode the team bus across Florida on his way to a B-team exhibition game he voiced his frustration to second-string catcher Norm Sherry, brother of 1959 World Series hero, Larry. Knowing Koufax was scheduled to pitch that day, Sherry made a suggestion. "Why not have some fun today. Don't try to throw so hard

**Opposite:** The Old Perfesser, Casey Stengel, managed the Yanks to ten pennants in 12 years.

and use more curve balls and change-ups."

Maybe the informal and pressureless atmosphere of the B game was just what the doctor or, in this case, Norm Sherry ordered. Koufax relaxed, and even though not throwing as hard, he suddenly realized that he could still throw just as fast. There was more bite on his curveball, and, above all, he wasn't wild.

During the next six seasons, Sandy Koufax would be as overpowering and dominating a pitcher as ever lived. Though he would continue to be dogged by injury and bad luck – bad enough to force him into premature retirement at the age of 31 – he would set a slew of records, pitch four no hitters, one of them a perfect game, and win the Cy Young Award three times. And all because he finally decided to relax.

In 1961 Koufax would compile an 18-13 record, including a league-leading 269 strike-

**Top:** Ralph Houk replaced Stengel as the Yankee skipper in 1961, promptly winning three more flags.

**Above:** Dodger Manager Walt Alston and his young lefty, Sandy Koufax, in 1961. The speedy southpaw was about to emerge as the National League's best pitcher.

**Above:** Roberto Clemente of the Pirates won four batting titles, had a .317 lifetime average and 3000 hits, despite having his career cut short when he was killed in a plane crash in 1972.

and Bob Purkey. And when they got contributions from the others starters and role players, well, that put them right in the thick of it.

As the pennant race heated up there were some great individual achievements. On 30 April Willie Mays reminded everyone that he was still one of the very best when he tied a record by belting four homers in a game. Later, the great Warren Spahn would become the third pitcher in National League history to win 300 games. And, in the dubious distinction department, the Philadelphia Phillies set a record for futility when they lost an incredible 23 games in a row.

While all this was happening in the senior circuit the American League was producing some surprises of its own. It wasn't the pennant race: that was over before it began. Under new manager Ralph Houk the New York Yankees were a powerhouse. Pitcher Whitey Ford was off to the greatest season of his career, and the moundwork behind him was solid. But it was still power that drove the team, power that would find the 1961 Yanks compared to the 1927 version of the team, the Ruth-Gehrig aggregation known as Murderers' Row.

Yogi Berra, Bill Skowron, Elston Howard and John Blanchard would all blast more than 20 round-trippers before the season ended, with more circuits from the likes of Hector Lopez, Clete Boyer and Tony Kubek. But the two players who really captured the imagination of the entire baseball world were the M & M boys, Mickey Mantle and Roger Maris. In 1961 they would make history.

The two sluggers had been a formidable combination in 1960, Mantle winning the home run crown, with 40, and Maris a notch behind, with 39. But that still didn't foreshadow what would happen in 1961. Mantle, of course, was still the big favorite, the home-grown Yankee who followed in the tradition of Ruth, Gehrig and DiMaggio, a switch hitter who belted long, high, majestic home runs much in the manner of the Babe. Maris, on the other hand, had come over from Kansas City in a trade, and the fans didn't look on him as a traditional Yankee. A lefthanded batter, he had a short, compact swing perfectly suited for the rightfield porch at Yankee Stadium. Many of his homers were line shots that just went into the lower stands. He didn't give the impression of the traditional baseball slugger.

When Maris got off to a very slow start in April, hitting around .200, with just a single home run, many thought his MVP prize of a year earlier wouldn't be repeated. Mantle already have seven circuits, and the rest of the team was also clubbing the ball. But in May Maris began coming alive. He closed the month with four homers in three days, to trail Mantle by two,

outs, and would help keep the Dodgers in the pennant race most of the way. The Braves were there too, and so were the Giants. That didn't surprise anyone. But two other things did. First, the defending world champion Pirates took a nosedive. Despite the fact that Roberto Clemente was driving towards his first battling title, the Bucs would be out of it early and finish a surprising sixth, four games below .500.

As big a surprise as the descent of the Pirates was the ascent of the Cincinnati Reds. The Reds, under manager Fred Hutchinson, had finished a dismal sixth in 1960, their record being an unimpressive 67-87. It seemed inconceivable that they could turn it around so quickly, yet here they were battling the favored teams in the early going.

Maybe, however, their low finish in 1960 had been misleading, for the core of the team was solid. To begin with, the Redlegs had a pair of genuine stars. Frank Robinson was already one of the best all-around players in the league, and young centerfielder Vada Pinson wasn't very far behind. The team has some other hard-hitters in first baseman Gordy Coleman and outfielder Wally Post. They had also developed a pitching staff, with a big three of Joey Jay, Jim O'Toole

**Left:** Base-stealing champ Lou Brock was one of the best all-around players in the National League and is a member of the Baseball Hall of Fame.

**Below:** Though he is swinging a couple of bats here, Whitey Ford did most of his work with his left arm. The Yanks' "Chairman of the Board" finished his Hall of Fame career with 236 wins.

14-12. And when both sluggers got red hot in June the excitement began building. Now some people began asking a disturbing question: was it possible that either of the M & M boys might break Babe Ruth's longstanding season record of 60 home runs?

The Babe had set his mark in 1927. Since then there had been only a couple of serious challenges. Both Jimmie Foxx, in 1932, and Hank Greenberg, in 1938, had slammed 58. But no one had come closer, and no one had really challenged the Babe since Greenberg. Ruth's standard was thus one of baseball's most sacred records, set by a man often looked upon as larger than life.

That's why the pressure started building, especially for Maris. Many people didn't want to see Ruth's record broken by anyone, but as far as New York fans were concerned, if it had to be

**Opposite:** The power of Mickey Mantle can be seen as he blasts his 45th home run in 1961.

**Top:** Roger Maris breaks one of baseball's most sacred records with his 61st homer.

**Above:** Commissioner of Baseball Ford Frick was the man who made the famous "asterisk" ruling.

done they wanted it done by Mantle, the "real" Yankee. To add even more pressure, Commissioner Ford Frick's office announced that unless the record was broken within the team's first 154 games (remember, the schedule had been increased to 162 in 1961), there would be an asterisk placed alongside it. Many felt that was unfair, that a record should be a record. Both Mantle and Maris began to field questions regularly about the record and the asterisk.

"I didn't even get involved in the debate," Maris said. "I still wasn't even thinking record. I just wanted to do my best and help the Yankees win another pennant."

The questions didn't stop because the two players wouldn't stop hitting home runs. Mantle slammed three homers in Washington, to again take the lead, 36-35, and he continued to hold the lead into August. Then Maris got hot again. He belted four homers in four days, to tie the race at 45. A few days later he found himself leading Mantle 48-45. Both sluggers were ahead of Ruth's pace, which made it even more difficult for them to hide from the growing publicity. For Maris, an intensely private and sometimes withdrawn man, the commotion over the race became especially disconcerting. "It became difficult for either of us to deny that the record was on our minds," he said. "In fact, it was on everyone's mind. We got no rest from it."

So while the Yankees raced toward still another American League flag the M & M boys raced toward immortality by challenging the Babe. But it was Maris who kept the lead. When he had 51, Mantle had 46. When Roger hit 53, the Mick was at 48. And still the media attention grew. "I was getting embarrassed by it all," Maris said. "We had a lot of other guys having good years. Why not give them some attention?"

That was true, but the M & M boys had by now become a national obsession. Mantle hit his 52nd on 8 September, and Maris slammed his 56th a day later. They had already become the first teammates to go over 50 in the same season, and

now that they had 108 they topped the record of 107 hit by Ruth and Gehrig in 1927. When Moose Skowron belted a homer shortly after that, it was the Yanks' 222nd of the year, breaking the record of the 1947 Giants and the 1956 Redlegs.

In the team's 151st game Maris hit his 58th. Mantle was stalled at 53, and it was obvious now that Maris was the man. The pressure on Maris had become so great that his hair began falling out in chunks. Yet he said the only place he could relax was on the ballfield: all he had to do there was hit.

He hit number 59 in the team's 154th game, so if he broke the record he'd have to live with the asterisk. He had another eight games left. Mantle cracked his 54th at Boston, but then a sudden illness put him on the bench. Maris continued his quest. He slammed his 60th off Jack Fisher of Baltimore, and there were still four games left. But in the next three he was shut out. Then came the finale against Boston.

Facing righthander Tracy Stallard in the fourth inning, Maris got his pitch and swung. Like so many others, the ball rocketed into the lower right field stands. It was number 61. He had done it.

"I couldn't even think as I went around the bases," he would say, later. "I was in a fog. I was all fogged out from a very, very hectic season and an extremely difficult month."

A difficult month for Maris, but a great year for the Yanks. As a team, the Bombers set a new mark, with 240 homers. They finished with a 109-53 record to win the pennant by a comfortable eight games over a good Detroit team that had won 101. Maris had hit only .269, but his 61 homers and 142 runs batted in won him a second Most Valuable Player Award. Mantle hit .317 and drove home 128 to go with his 54 homers.

Many of the Yanks had outstanding seasons, including pitcher Ford, who would take the Cy Young Award with an incredible 25-4 year. The batting champ was Norm Cash of Detroit, who hit a career best .361. And it was a year for the sluggers all over the league. Besides Maris and Mantle, others dented the fences all season long. Killebrew of Minnesota and Jim Gentile of Baltimore slammed 46, Rocky Colavito had 45 and Cash had 41 to go with his batting title.

There had been so much excitement that not much was written about expansion, but it was successful, even if the new teams were not. The new Washington Senators wound up tied for last

with the KC Athletics at 61-100. The new Los Angeles Angels team was only a notch above, at 70-91. But that was to be expected. Meanwhile, expansion was here to stay.

In the National League, where a good pennant race was overshadowed by the Maris-Mantle explosion, there was a surprise winner for the second straight year. The Cincinnati Reds had hung on to win by four games over the Dodgers. Cincy finished up with a 93-61 record in the wake of some fine individual performances. Frank Robinson, though not leading the league in any major hitting category, batted .323 and was named the league's Most Valuable Player. Vada Pinson had a career-best .343, while Joey Jay won 21 games, Jim O'Toole 19 and Bob Purkey 16. Other members of the team turned in fine years to help bring the flag to Cincinnati and tiny Crosley Field.

There were also a number of familiar names dominating the league. As mentioned earlier, Warren Spahn, at age 40, had won 21 games, as well as the 300th of his great career. Young Koufax had found himself with 18 victories. The batting title went to Clemente, while Orlando Cepeda of the Giants led the loop with 46 homers and 142 runs batted in. The Rookie of

**Above:** Yankee Whitey Ford set a record 33 2/3 straight scoreless innings in World Series play.

the Year was a sweet-swinging outfielder with the Cubs, Billy Williams, who hit .278 and who would go on to a long career that would land him in the Hall of Fame. So it had been a great year in the National League as well.

In a sense, the 1961 World Series was almost an anticlimax. So much had already happened, and the Yanks went in as overwhelming favorites. This time the Bombers didn't disappoint. They won the first game 2-0 behind Ford, then lost the second to Joey Jay 6-2. But after that they romped by scores of 3-2, 7-0 and 13-5 to take the championship in five games. No team could touch the Bronx Bombers in '61.

The Series also saw another great record being broken. During the regular season Babe Ruth had lost his homer mark to Roger Maris. In the Series the redoubtable Bambino saw one of his pitching marks fall. Ruth, of course, had been an outstanding hurler with the Red Sox before coming to the Yanks and swinging the bat. He had set a record of 29 2/3 consecutive scoreless innings in World Series play. Against Cincinnati, Whitey Ford broke it. He had started the string of goose eggs against Pittsburgh the year before, and in the 1961 he threw more blanks at the Reds and wound up with 32 straight scoreless frames. He would extend the mark to 33 and 2/3 before it stopped. It was another example of an outstanding individual performance in a landmark year.

The first big news of 1962 was that Casey Stengel had come back to baseball. The beloved former skipper of the Yankees, who had been fired for being too old two years earlier, was now reunited with his old boss, George Weiss. Both men returned to run one of the National League's expansion franchises – the one in New

York, of course. It was officially the New York Metropolitans, but it would be known to one and all as the New York Mets. It would play its first season in the antiquated but historical Polo Grounds, once the home of the New York Giants.

Expansion team number two brought major league baseball to Texas. The first Lone Star State ballclub was in Houston and was originally called the Colt 45's (later to be changed to the Astros). Veteran baseball man Harry Craft was named as its first manager.

Now both leagues had 10 teams and a 162-game schedule. Major league baseball's first expansion in some 60 years was complete, and the game stretched from coast to coast in each league. When it was time to play ball, however, everyone figured the New York Yankees would still have a lock on the AL. The team seemed loaded, with hitting, pitching and the M & M boys.

The National League , on the other hand, was expected to be a dogfight. Both the Dodgers and Giants looked strong, as did the Reds, Pirates, Braves and Cards. And, in fact, those five would really beat up on the Colt 45's, the Cubs and especially the Mets. The New Yorkers would lose 120 games in their initial season, prompting Stengel to utter his now-famous plea for help: "Can't anyone here play this game?" Ol' Case shouted on more than one occasion. He is also credited with coining the phrase "The Amazin' Mets," a name that stayed even when the team finally became a winner.

Early in the season the pennant race had to take a back seat to another great individual event. The great Stan Musial, still playing for the Cards at the age of 41, banged out his 3431st hit, enabling The Man to pass the immortal Honus Wagner as the all-time hit leader in National League history. Musial would go on to hit .330 in 1962, banging out 19 homers and driving home 82 runs. His career had begun the year Pearl Harbor was attacked, 1941, yet more than 20 years later he could still swing the bat with the best of them.

The pennant race in the senior circuit evolved into a three-team fight among the Dodgers, Giants and Reds. Cincinnati proved its win a year earlier was no fluke. Frank Robinson was on his way to a .342 season, and pitchers Bob Purkey and Joey Jay would each win more than 20 games (23 and 21, respectively). The Giants would have a 24-game winner in Jack Sanford, as well as a power team featuring the likes of Mays, Cepeda, McCovey and Filipe Alou. The ballclub would hit 204 home runs during the season.

By contrast, the Dodgers were a team of speed and pitching. Big Don Drysdale and Sandy Kou-

**Above:** New York City says hello to old friend Casey Stengel and the New York Mets, a new NL franchise in 1962.

**Left:** Dodger Stadium in Los Angeles was usually the scene of a packed house.

**Left:** The Cards' Stan Musial sets a new NL record with 3431 hits at Dodger Stadium on May 19, 1962. The "Man" would finish his career with 3630 basehits.

**Right:** Shortstop Maury Wills of the Dodgers would top Ty Cobb's record for stolen bases (96) in 1962 by stealing 104.

fax were the best one-two punch in the league, while shortstop Wills and young centerfielder Willie Davis could dazzle on the basepaths. Brooklyn-born outfielder Tommy Davis, though not a bona fide power hitter, was batting well over .300 and knocking in runs at a league-leading clip.

It appeared that any one of the three teams was capable of winning the flag, yet some individual performances nearly overshadowed the exciting pennant race. During the first half of the season it began to look as if Sandy Koufax was becoming the best pitcher in the league. By 30 June, when he took the mound against the lowly New York Mets, he already had a 10-4 record. Nine innings later he had his first no-hitter and 13 strikeouts. But there was a problem. Koufax had broken an artery in the fleshy part of his hand a short time earlier, and the injury had begun to affect the circulation in his left index finger. Even when he no-hit the Mets, there was little or no feeling in the finger.

Yet three more victories followed, running Koufax' record to a superb, 14-4. But then the blood circulation to the finger stopped completely. For a short time, it was questionable if the lefthander would even keep the finger. The injury put Koufax on the shelf and really hurt the Dodgers' pennant chances. Sandy came back to

try three late-season starts, but the finger still wasn't sound, and he lost all three. That left Koufax with a 14-7 record, 216 strikeouts in 184 innings and a league-leading 2.54 ERA. Without the injury, he surely would have gone well over 20 victories.

There was another Dodger, however, who wasn't slowing down. Shortstop Maury Wills, just a few months short of his 30th birthday, was challenging one of baseball's longest-standing records, Ty Cobb's single-season stolen base mark of 96, set back in 1915. Though not possessed of blazing speed, Wills was a fiery competitor who studied the pitchers and used a variety of different slides to swipe his sacks. He and Willie Davis, at the top of the lineup, set the table for the likes of Tommy Davis and Frank Howard.

Despite being bruised and battered by pounding down the basepaths all over the league, Wills tied Cobb's mark in 156 games, the same number of games (because of two ties) that Cobb had played in 1915. Then, in the final nine games of the year, he pilfered eight more bags and set a new all-time mark of 104 steals.

There were nine more games for a good reason. The Giants and Dodgers finished the season in a dead tie, with 101-61 records. Cincinnati, at 98-64, gave it a run but wound up three games back. Now the two rivals would once again engage in a best-of-three playoff, just like 1951. But instead of a subway ride, as was the case in New York, this was a freeway playoff, fans taking the California freeways from one park to the other.

The playoffs must have had an eerie ring for longtime Dodger fans who had followed the club to the West Coast. The teams split the first two games, the Giants winning 8-0, then the Dodgers coming from behind to win the second 8-7. In the deciding contest the Dodgers took a 4-2 lead into the ninth inning. (In 1951 they had a 4-1 margin going into the ninth.) Once again the Giants rallied, pushing across four runs, to win the game, the series and the pennant 6-4.

The two clubs also dominated the individual titles. Tommy Davis was the batting champ, at .346, and also led in RBIs, with an amazing 153. Mays, however, took the home run crown, with 49, and also drove home 141 runs while hitting .304. Jack Sanford of the Giants went 24-7, but Don Drysdale at 25-9 won the Cy Young Award and led the league in strikeouts, with 232. Wills, with his 104 thefts, was the MVP.

As was the case back in 1951, the Giants would be meeting the New York Yankees in the World Series. The Yanks had won by five games, but they were not the same powerhouse they had

**Above:** Maury Wills begins his slide as the Pirates' Dick Groat waits for the throw. As usual, Wills will make it.

**Opposite:** The Giants' Chuck Hiller has just hit a grand slam homer off Marshall Bridges of the Yanks in the 1962 World Series.

**Opposite below:** The Yankees' Ralph Terry was the pitching star of the '62 World Series.

**Above:** Willie Mays swats an opposite-field homer in a crucial playoff game against the Dodgers in 1962.

**Below:** Tom Tresh of the Yankees watches his three-run homer sail into the seats during the 1962 World Series against the Giants.

been the year before. No one should have expected Roger Maris to hit 61 home runs again, or even come close. He was an excellent ballplayer, but not a great one. He had had to settle for 33 homers in 1962, and a .256 batting average. Mantle had fallen victim to his old bugaboo, the injury. Yet playing in just 123 games, the Mick hit .321, walloped 30 homers and drove home 89 runs. So despite missing nearly 40 games, Mantle was named the league's MVP for the third time.

But the M & M boys had had some help. Young Ralph Terry won 23 games, while Ford took 17. Shortstop-outfielder Tom Tresh batted a strong .286 and was named Rookie of the Year. And while Yogi Berra was winding down his great career, Elston Howard was coming to the peak of his. Thus the team was still strong enough to win.

Some of the biggest surprises had come from the teams chasing them. The powerful Minnesota Twins, the franchise that had come from Washington just a few years earlier, finished second at 91-71. And the Los Angeles Angels, an expansion team only the year before, shocked everyone with a third-place 86-76 finish under Bill Rigney. Veteran Pete Runnels of Boston won his second batting title, at .326, while Killebrew was the homer king, with 48, and the RBI leader, with 126.

Now all eyes focused on the Series. It opened in San Francisco, with Ford and Billy O'Dell as the opposing pitchers. The Yanks got a pair in the first, and in the second the Giants ended Ford's record scoreless streak of 33 innings by pushing across a tally. They got another in the third, to tie the game, and it stayed that way until the seventh. Then the Yanks got four runs in the final three frames to win it easily, 6-2. One irony was that former Yankee Series hero Don Larsen made an appearance in relief for the Giants.

In a game-two battle of aces Jack Sanford bested Ralph Terry 2-0, throwing a three-hitter and allowing his ballclub to even the Series. Then came a day off for the long trip to New York, following which New York sent 14-game winner Bill Stafford to the mound against former American League star Billy Pierce, who had won 16 times during the regular season.

This one was also low-scoring, as the pitching continued to dominate. It was scoreless for 6½ innings, and then the Yanks struck. Maris drove in a pair with a single and eventually came around to score the third run. A two-run homer by Ed Bailey in the ninth made it close, but the Yanks had won 3-2, to again take the lead in games.

Game four saw the Giants start young Juan Marichal, a native of the Dominican Republic, who had won 18 games in the regular season. Marichal was on the brink of becoming one of the great pitchers of his generation and was fully capable of beating the Yanks, who countered with Ford. But neither was around at the finish. Marichal was injured attempting to bunt in the fifth inning and left the game. It was settled in the seventh, when Giants' second baseman Chuck Hiller broke a 2-2 tie by becoming the first National Leaguer to hit a grand slam homer in World Series competition. It came off reliever Marshall Bridges and paved the way for a 7-3 San Francisco victory.

The fifth-game tiebreaker went to Terry and the Yanks over Sanford and the Giants, a game iced by a Tom Tresh three-run homer in the eighth. The final was 5-3, and as the two teams flew back to San Francisco the Yankees needed just one more victory to be World Champions.

They sent Whitey Ford to the mound to face Billy Pierce. The two southpaws had pitched some epic battles when Pierce was with the White Sox, so they were not strangers to each other. This time Pierce got the better of the fray. San Francisco got three in the fourth and two in the fifth, to break it open. Maris homered for the Yanks, but Pierce wound up with a brilliant three-hitter and a 5-2 victory for his team. That brought it all down to a single game. Houk went with 23-game winner Terry, while Giants' man-

**Opposite:** Willie McCovey of the Giants watches a ball during the third game of the 1962 World Series. He would end the Series with a hard line drive to Bobby Richardson in the seventh game.

**Left:** Bobby Richardson avoids Orlando Cepeda's spikes as he fires to first in a doubleplay try during '62 Series.

ager Al Dark countered with Jack Sanford.

It turned out to be a classic. Both pitchers were primed for the occasion and wouldn't yield a thing for the first four innings. Then, in the top of the fifth, Bill Skowron and Clete Boyer both singled, putting runners on first and third. Sanford then walked opposing pitcher Terry, and leadoff hitter Tony Kubek stepped up. Kubek slapped a grounder to short, and the Giants went for the doubleplay, conceding the run. They must have felt their big hitters would get to Terry, but they didn't, and going to the bottom of the ninth, the Yanks still had that slim 1-0 lead.

Just three outs away, Terry went to work. But Matty Alou led off by bunting for a basehit. Then Terry got a second wind, striking out Filipe Alou and Hiller. The next batter was Willie Mays. The Say Hey Kid wasn't about to give up. He lined a shot into the right centerfield gap as Alou raced around second. Only a great effort by Maris to cut the ball off prevented the run from scoring. But now the Giants had men on second and third, with the powerful Willie McCovey coming to bat.

Manager Houk decided to stick with right-hander Terry, and despite the fact that first base was open, they opted to pitch to McCovey. The strategy almost backfired on the first pitch when the big guy slammed a long drive to right, but it was foul. He then took the next pitch for a ball. Terry cranked and pitched again. McCovey

swung and sent a hard liner toward right, but second baseman Bobby Richardson somehow reached up and caught it before it rocketed into the outfield. The Series was over, and by the length of a glove it was the Yankees, not the Giants, who had won.

It was a strange series in that many of the big bats were stiffled. Maris hit just .174, Mantle hit .120 and the Yanks batted only .199 as a team. Mays hit a modest .250, without a homer and with just one RBI. McCovey hit .200 and Cepeda .158. So it didn't go as expected, but then it seldom does, which is one of the reasons we all love the game so much.

**Above:** Willie Mays heads back to third after a pickoff try by Whitey Ford of the Yanks. Mays was safe.

# CHAPTER IX
# END OF AN ERA

The 1961 season saw Ted
Williams in a new role, that of a
batting coach.

In a sense, the 1961 and 1962 seasons were something of a beginning, with four new teams completing baseball's first major expansion in more than a half century. But the 1963 and 1964 seasons seemed to have more than their share of endings. More and more players linked to the earlier decade of the 1940s were bowing out, and, to the surprise of many, the reign of one of the sport's greatest dynasties was also coming to an end.

Veteran pitcher Early Wynn, who had led the White Sox to a pennant in 1959, was rapidly approaching the end of the line. In 1962 Wynn had a 7-15 record with the Sox. That gave him 299 victories for his career. The portly right-hander desperately wanted number 300, but the White Sox released him during spring training in 1963. At first it looked as if no one wanted him, but several weeks into the season his old team, the Cleveland Indians, signed him to pitch.

Five times the old man trudged to the mound in quest of that one elusive victory. Four times he failed, but on the fifth try he finally got it. With relief help from Jerry Walker, Wynn defeated the As 7-4. It was the only game he'd win all year, but it was number 300.

Another veteran didn't have quite the same struggle. Stan Musial, who had played only for the Cardinals in his long career, announced that 1963 would be his last year. The Man had been a great player for so long, setting so many records along the way, that it seemed hard to believe.

**Above:** Pete Rose was NL Rookie of the Year in 1963. His all-out style of play from day one earned him the nickname "Charley Hustle."

**Left:** Rose was a switch-hitter who loved the game and would finish his great career as baseball's all-time hit leader, at 4256.

Known for, among other things, his crouching, peek-a-boo stance, Stan the Man was a popular figure who would be missed, and many fans came out around the league to see him play one more time.

But there were plenty of good younger players around now. The Cincinnati Reds had a rookie second baseman, a stocky, hustling kid with a crewcut who already had the nickname of Charlie Hustle. His name was Pete Rose, and before he finished he would get more base hits than any player in baseball history.

The Cardinals had a hard-throwing right-hander who was also beginning to assert himself in 1963. Bob Gibson would become one of the best of his time, a fierce competitor, a pitcher who loved the pressure of a big game and who was always at his best when the chips were down.

Over in the American League a young outfielder with the Boston Red Sox was beginning to make a name in his own right. He had pressure, too, because he was trying to fill the shoes of another all-time great. Carl Yastrzemski had joined the Red Sox as a 21-year-old in 1961. He was immediately presented with the leftfield job, since it had been vacated the year before by one Theodore Samuel Williams. There was only one Splendid Splinter, but Yaz plugged away, and in 1963 he was making a run at his first American League batting title.

The Baltimore Orioles had a huge first baseman named John "Boob" Powell who was also finding himself as a slugger by 1963. There were others, of course, who would go on and make their names during the 1960s and into the 1970s, and there were still more just over the horizon.

As for the pennant race in the junior circuit, well, there really wasn't one. The Yankees took off fast, never looked back, and would wind up with 104 victories and a 10½ game bulge. But in a way, it seemed as if they were doing it with mirrors.

Yogi Berra was in his final year with the Yanks, and was reduced to a spot player who would be in just 64 games. Add to that injuries to both Mantle and Maris, limiting the two sluggers to 65 and 90 games respectively, and you had to wonder where the power was. Yet Ralph Houk kept the team winning big. Whitey Ford had another fine season, with a 24-7 record, and was joined by Jim Bouton, who won 21 games. Young Al Downing was 13-5, and Ralph Terry 17-15.

With Mantle and Maris hurting, the Bombers got a big contribution from catcher Elston Howard, who would be the American League MVP, as well as from young Joe Pepitone, who took over at first base, and from some of the other veterans like Kubek, Richardson, Boyer, Tresh and Blanchard. But even with the 104 wins and a

fourth straight pennant they obviously weren't the Bombers of old.

Except for Ford's pitching, the Yankees didn't dominate any of the individual statistical categories in 1963. Yastrzemski was the batting champ, at .321, while Killebrew repeated as home run champ, with 45, and Dick Stuart of Boston led the loop with 118 RBIs. All in all, it was a relatively quiet year in the American League.

Though the National League didn't have the down-to-the-wire pennant race of the year before, the senior circuit nevertheless had a brace of outstanding performances. For starters, there was Sandy Koufax. Completely recovered from the circulatory problem of the previous year, Koufax completed his metamorphosis from an erratic thrower to the best pitcher in the game. Dominant from beginning to end, Koufax brilliantly led the Dodgers to the NL flag. He won 25 games and lost just five, giving up only 214 hits in 311 innings. He threw his second no-hitter, led the majors with 306 strikeouts and posted a league-leading 1.88 earned run average. He was close to unbeatable.

Koufax wasn't the only pitcher to turn in a great year in the senior circuit. Juan Marichal of the Giants completed the first of four straight 20-game seasons, finishing at 25-8. He and Koufax would have some epic duels over the next few years. And there was more. Warren Spahn, at the age of 42 and just two years from retirement, turned in an incredible 23-7 season, giving him

**Above:** Pitcher Bob Gibson of the Cards was starting to hit his stride in 1963. He would win 251 games in an outstanding career which saw him remain a ferocious competitor and one of the great money pitchers.

350 career victories and 13 20-game campaigns.

Jim Maloney of Cincinnati also won 23, and Dick Ellsworth of Chicago took 22. In fact, there were 10 20-game winners in the majors during 1963. Young Pete Rose was the Rookie of the Year, the first of many honors he would win. Tommy Davis of the Dodgers repeated as batting champ, with a .326 mark, while Hank Aaron and Willie McCovey shared home run title, with 44. Aaron drove home the most runs, with 130.

The Dodgers took the pennant by six games over the improving Cardinals and would resume their World Series rivalry with the Yanks for the first time since 1956. The Yanks had by now won 20 World Championships, six of them four-game sweeps. In all their appearances in the fall classic the Yanks had never lost in four straight. So perhaps the 1963 Series should have been seen as a foreshadowing, for the Dodgers simply used their great pitching to mow the Yankees down. Koufax started his first World Series game in the opener, and he was opposed by money pitcher Whitey Ford, one of the most successful postseason pitchers ever. But it was Koufax who did the job.

The lefty quickly showed the Yanks why he had become the scourge of the National League. He went out to the mound and promptly struck

out the first five Yankees he faced. At the same time, the Dodgers jumped all over Ford for four second-inning runs. They got another in the third, and that just about wrapped it up. Only a two-run homer by Tom Tresh in the eighth inning avoided the shutout. The Dodgers not only won the opener 5-2, but Koufax had set a new World Series mark by striking out 15 Yankees.

In the second game Johnny Podres bested Al Downing 4-1, and, with the Series moving from New York to Los Angeles, Don Drysdale pitched a brilliant three-hitter to defeat Jim Bouton and the Yanks 1-0. The Dodger run was driven in by Tommy Davis in the first inning on a bad-hop basehit. Now the Dodgers returned Koufax to the mound in the fourth game with the opportunity to sweep.

The Yanks had no choice but to come back with their best, Whitey Ford. With nearly 56,000 fans jammed into Dodger Stadium, Koufax and Ford went to work. This time both pitchers had it. The game remained scoreless through four and a half innings. Then, in the bottom of the fifth, big Frank Howard hit a mammoth 430-foot homer and gave his team a 1-0 lead. It stayed that way until the top of the seventh, when Mantle, flashing his only muscle of the Series, slammed a long homer to tie the game.

But the Dodgers wasted no time getting it back. In their half of the inning Jim Gilliam led

off by bouncing one to Clete Boyer at third. First baseman Joe Pepitone lost the throw in a background of white shirts, and the ball rolled down the rightfield line, Gilliam scampering around to third. On Ford's next pitch Willie Davis lofted a sacrifice fly to Mantle in center, and Gilliam came home with the go-ahead run. That was all Koufax needed. He retired the Yanks in the eighth and ninth, competing the 2-1 victory and the Dodgers' four-game sweep. Ford had been brilliant in defeat, yielding just two hits, but the Yankees' luck had finally run out.

Yankee bats were also strangely silent. In four games against the Dodgers the Bombers hit just .171 as a team, scoring just four runs. Mantle batted a mere .133, and Maris went hitless in five at bats before being injured in the second game.

There were two questions on many minds after the season. One was, could the New Yorkers regroup and win again? And the other was, just how good would Sandy Koufax get?

One final note about the 1963 season. On 29 September Stan Musial cracked a double in a game against Cincinnati. It would be The Man's 3630th basehit, and his last. He would retire from the game with a .331 lifetime batting average, seven batting crowns and 475 home runs. Like that of Ted Williams, his career had been a great one from beginning to end.

Both New York teams were in the news before the 1964 season began. Ralph Houk, who had managed the Yankees to three straight pennants and two World Series triumphs since taking over from Casey Stengel, announced that he would be

**Above:** Warren Spahn, at 42, won 23 games. The Braves gave him a "Spahnie Night."

**Right:** Sandy Koufax, mobbed by Dodger teammates after completing a World Series sweep of Yankees in 1963.

**Opposite top:** Righty Jim Bouton won 21 games, which helped the Yankees to win another pennant in 1963.

**Opposite bottom:** Sandy Koufax was 25-5 in 1963, with 306 strikeouts and a 1.88 earned run average. There was little doubt that he had become baseball's best pitcher.

**Above:** Stan "The Man" Musial greets fans at the start of his final season in 1963.

**Right:** Yankee great Yogi Berra became the team's new manager in 1964.

moving upstairs to become team's general manager. Taking his place on the field would be none other than the ever-popular Yogi Berra, who had retired as a player after the 1963 season. Yogi was in a tough spot, trying to become the boss just a few months after being one of the guys.

Across town the Mets were ready to move into their brand new ballpark in Queens. After two years in the old Polo Grounds they were moving to Shea Stadium, but there was little hope for much improvement in the standings. After losing 120 times during their first campaign, they had dropped 111 games in their second season. The star of the team continued to be Manager Stengel, now one of baseball's most beloved elder statesmen, a walking-talking testament to the game's grand past.

The game's present was represented by a pair of great pennant races, each of which went down to the wire. In the National League the biggest surprise was the off year of the Dodgers. They still had Koufax and Drysdale, Maury Wills and the two Davis's, as well as a number of other fine players. But for some reason the team played in a funk except when Koufax was pitching, and never really figured in the action.

It was the Philadelphia Phillies who got off fast in 1964. Led by a rookie third baseman named Richie Allen, who hit for both power and aver-

age, the Phils surprised everyone and quickly built a sizable lead in the race. The rest of the league began chasing them. St Louis, Cincinnati, the Giants and the Braves all seemed to have a chance, but only if the Phils would come back to the rest of the pack.

To many, the Cardinals had the best chance. St Louis was building a fine team with a number of outstanding players. They had veteran shortstop Dick Groat, obtained in a trade with Pittsburgh, and he played alongside third sacker Ken Boyer, the brother of the Yankees' Clete and a much better hitter. Bill White was an outstanding first baseman, and Curt Flood was one of the best centerfielders in the league. Young Tim McCarver was an improving catcher, and Mike Shannon provided some power in right. The pitching staff was led by righthander Gibson and lefties Ray Sadecki and Curt Simmons. But something was still missing. And on 15 June the Cards and Cubs made one of those trades that wound up changing baseball history.

It was announced that St Louis had swapped pitcher Ernie Broglio, who had won 21 games back in 1960 and 18 in 1963, to the Cubs for outfielder Lou Brock. Brock had come up to the Cubs in 1962, hitting .263 that year. But he had batted just .258 the next season and was hitting only .251 at the time of the trade, some 52 games into the season. Brock had a world of natural speed and had flashed a good bat on occasion. The problem was that Brock thought he should hit home runs. That's where the money was, he reasoned, and after once hitting a mammoth 460-foot shot into the centerfield seats in the old

**Above:** The NY Mets moved to brand-new Shea Stadium in 1964, and the old Polo Grounds were torn down to make room for apartments.

**Left:** Curt Flood of the Cards was an outstanding player in the 1960s. But he will be always remembered as the man who challenged baseball's long-standing reserve clause. The final result of his sacrifice was free agency.

Polo Grounds he was convinced he was right.

Because of that, he hadn't improved as a ballplayer . . . until he went to the Cards. Then, presto! Manager Johnny Keane told Brock he was his everyday leftfielder and would be batting second in the order. Knowing at last what his role

was meant everything to Brock. He forgot about home runs and concentrated on basehits and on wreaking havoc on the basepaths.

"I finally realized I didn't have the physical makeup to be a consistent power hitter," Brock confessed. "So I had to make a choice. Do I go and try to develop myself as a power hitter or do I become a pest on the basepaths?"

Suddenly Lou Brock became a different kind of ballplayer, one of the best in the National League. In 103 games for the Cards he batted .348 and stole 33 bases. His season totals would include 43 steals and a .315 batting average, as well as an accumulation of 200 hits. And that was only a beginning. Lou Brock would go on to become baseball's all-time basestealing king and a member of the 3000 hit club. He would eventually be elected to the Hall of Fame. And it all started because of a midseason trade.

With Brock doing his thing for the Cards, they became a complete team and began chasing the Phils in earnest. But there were also some other things happening. On 21 June Jim Bunning of the Phillies tossed a perfect game against the New York Mets, the first in modern National League history. And by August another pitcher was again in the news.

Sandy Koufax was on his way to proving that 1963 was no accident. He had already thrown his third no-hitter and was the dominant pitcher in the league. Then, on 8 August, he dove back into second base on a pickoff attempt and landed hard on his left elbow. After the game it was very sore. But on 20 August Koufax was back on the mound throwing a shutout against the Cardinals and striking out 13. His record was 19-5, and he was just a game away from another 20-game sea-

son. That night he went to sleep as usual, but when he awoke the next morning he was stunned by what he found.

"I had to drag my arm out of bed like a log," he recalled. "It looked like a water-logged log. Where it had been swollen outside the joint before, it was now swollen all the way from the shoulder down to the wrist – inside, outside, everywhere. For an elbow, I had a knee; that's how thick it was."

After a series of tests, the doctors determined that Koufax was suffering from traumatic arthritis in the elbow, brought on by the wear and tear of pitching. The worst news was that the condition would not get better and would probably get worse.

So Sandy Koufax would miss the rest of the year. After that he had to skip throwing between starts. He would continue for two more years, putting together his most brilliant seasons, including 382 strikeouts in 1965 and records of 26-8 and 27-9. He would also throw a perfect game against the Cubs in 1965. But the elbow never would get better, and, fearing permanent disability, Koufax would retire after the 1966 season at the age of 31. But for a five-year period he was one of the most dominant pitchers who ever lived.

The season ended with an incredible finish. With 12 games left, the Phillies still held a 6½ game lead on the Cardinals. Then the Phils promptly went out and lost 10 straight. Nothing they did worked. The Cardinals crept closer and closer, winning eight straight at one point and then taking the pennant by one game. Philadelphia tied for second with Cincinnati, the Reds also coming very close to winning.

Ken Boyer, the St Louis third baseman, was the MVP, batting .295 and leading the league with 119 RBIs. Roberto Clemente took another batting title, with a .329 mark, while the Say Hey

Kid, Willie Mays, walloped 47 home runs. (A year later he would hit 52.) Wills still led the league in steals, with 53, but it wouldn't be long before Lou Brock became the main man on the basepaths. Larry Jackson of the Cubs had 24 victories, best in the league, while Marichal won 21, and Sedecki of the Cards 20.

In the American League the Yankees were

**Top:** Willie Mays about to get the 2000th hit of his career in 1963.

**Above:** Mickey Mantle was still a top slugger in the early 1960s.

**Above:** Whitey Ford shown shutting out the Orioles on July 15, 1964.

pitching was spotty, and the bombers were being challenged.

Chicago and Baltimore were both in the thick of the pennant fight. Brooks Robinson was having a great season and had become one of the fine all-round players in the league. Just past midseason Ford began having some hip problems, and the team had fallen to third place. So the Yanks went down to the farm and brought up a 22-year-old righthander named Mel Stottlemyre, who did what Ford himself had done back in 1950 – lifted a sagging pitching staff.

Stottlemyre won his first game over Chicago and went on to compile a 9-3 mark the rest of the year. With the bats picking up again, the Yanks somehow managed to squeak to the flag, finishing at 99-63, topping the White Sox by a game and the Orioles by two. It took some strong individual seasons to do it. Mantle finished with a .303 average, 35 homers and 111 RBIs. Catcher Howard hit .313 with 84 ribbys.

There were also some other happenings around the league. The Twins had a rookie outfielder named Tony Oliva, a native Cuban, who came in swinging a mean bat. Oliva led the league in batting from the beginning. He won the crown, with a .323 average, and was named Rookie of the year for his efforts. He went on to a fine career, one that would have been even better if he had not fallen victim to bad knees.

Oliva's teammate, Harmon Killebrew, took

having problems. The team looked sluggish, even though Mickey Mantle was putting together a very good season and Elston Howard continued to excel. Roger Maris was also hitting for a better average than usual, but he just wasn't the power hitter he had been a few years earlier. Whitey Ford was on the way to 17 victories, and Jim Bouton would win 18. But beyond that, the

**Above left:** Young Tim McCarver of the Cards blasts a three-run homer to win the fifth game of the 1964 World Series for the Cards over the Yanks.

**Left:** Bob Gibson bears down in fifth-game action during the 1964 World Series. Gibson would also win the seventh, deciding game.

**Above:** As shadows engulf Yankee Stadium, Ken Boyer of the Cardinals belts the grand-slam home run that won the fourth game of the '64 Series for St Louis.

his third straight home run crown, belting 49 and firmly establishing himself as one of the top sluggers in the game. Brooks Robinson drove home the most runs, with 118, and Oliva led the circuit with 217 hits. Luis Aparicio took his ninth straight stolen base title, with 57. Gary Peters, who had been Rookie of the Year, with 19 victories in 1963, won 20 games for the White Sox in 1964.

So did Dean Chance, and he was an original. Chance was a 23-year-old righthander who came up with the LA Angels for good in 1962. He was 14-10 that year, but only 13-18 the next season. He was a free spirit, and the Angels worried that he spent too much time with another original, lefthander Bo Belinski, who had something of a reputation as a playboy.

Yet in 1964 Dean Chance put together one of the greatest seasons in years. He compiled a 20-9 record, and that included a phenomenal 1.65 earned run average and 11 shutouts. Chance had a few more good seasons, including a 20-gamer, but he never quite reached the heights of 1964 again. For his efforts, he was named the Cy Young Award winner for the year.

Now it was the time for the World Series, and the Yanks sought to regain the title many of them assumed was always theirs. As usual, the Bombers called on Whitey Ford in the opener at Busch Stadium in St Louis, the Cards countered with Ray Sedecki. The Yanks, though playing without their injured shortstop, Tony Kubek, nevertheless took a 3-2 lead after two innings and extended it to 4-2 in the fifth. But the Cards exploded for four in the sixth, as Ford left the game with arm trouble, not to return for the remainder of the Series. St Louis went on to win the opener 9-5 and looked to be in excellent shape.

Game two had rookie Stottlemyre up against

**Above:** As shadows engulf Yankee Stadium, Ken Boyer of the Cardinals belts the grand-slam home run that won the fourth game of the '64 Series for St Louis.

the strong-armed Gibson. While Stottlemyre looked sharp in the early innings, Gibson appeared to be overpowering. The hard-throwing righthander fanned six Yanks in the first three innings. The Cards got a run in the bottom of the third and took the lead, but New York came back with one in the fourth and another in the sixth to go ahead 2-1. Then, in the seventh, they got to Gibson for two more and put the game away with four in the ninth. Stottlemyre, the rookie, went all the way for an 8-3 victory. So as the Series returned to New York, the Yanks seemed to have the advantage.

It was yet another pitcher's battle in game three, Jim Bouton hurling for the New Yorkers against Curt Simmons of the Cards. The game was tied at 1-1 in the ninth, and St Louis replaced Simmons with knuckleballer Barney Schultz. The first batter was Mantle, and the Mick promptly picked out a floater and belted it out of sight for a game-winning homer. It was the Switcher's 16th homer in World Series competition, enabling him to break a tie with Babe Ruth as the most prolific home run hitter in Series history. More important, it gave the Yanks a 2-1 lead in games and a chance to put the Cardinals away.

The Cards turned to Ray Sedecki once again in the fourth game. With Ford injured, the Yanks decided to go with lefthander Al Downing. It was a strange game in that all the runs were scored in just two innings. Sedecki, in fact, never made it past the first. The Yanks scored three times and looked to be on their way once more. But now the Cards got some great relief pitching, first by Roger Craig and then by Ron Taylor, and the three runs were all the Bombers would muster. Downing, meanwhile, shut the Cardinals down until the sixth, Then, with one out, the Cards got a pair of singles. Shortstop Dick Groat next hit what looked like a double play ball at second baseman Bobby Richardson. But he bobbled it for an error, and St Louis had the sacks loaded, with Ken Boyer up. The veteran third sacker whacked a grand slam homer, putting his team up by one run. And that's all the Cardinals needed to tie the Series at two games each.

The pivotal fifth game was a rematch between Gibson and Stottlemyre, and like their first matchup, both pitchers were sharp. But the Cards managed a pair of runs off the rookie righthander in the fifth, and Gibson made them stand up right into the bottom of the ninth. Then the Yankees began to rally.

Mantle led off and was safe on an error by Groat. Joe Pepitone then hit drive right back at Gibson. The ball glanced off the pitcher and began rolling toward third. Like a cat, Gibby bounced off the mound, grabbed the ball,

whirled and fired to first. His throw just nipped Pepitone as Mantle took second. The importance of the play was felt when the next batter, Tom Tresh, belted a homer into the rightfield stands. Had Gibson not nailed Pepitone, the game would have been over. Now it was tied at two, and after Gibson retired the Yanks, it went into the tenth inning.

The Cards wasted no time taking advantage of the break. Facing reliever Pete Mikkelsen in the tenth, catcher Tim McCarver belted a three-run shot that would win the game 5-2, giving St Louis a 3-2 advantage as the Series returned to Busch Stadium for game six.

In this one the Yanks looked like the Bronx Bombers of old. Maris and Mantle belted back-to-back homers in the sixth, and in the eighth Pepitone also whacked a grand slam, leading the Bombers to an 8-3 win behind Jim Bouton and sending the Series to a seventh game. With no tomorrows, both managers gambled. Mel Stottlemyre and Bob Gibson would be meeting for the third time, but now with only two days rest. The question was, which pitcher would be stronger?

For three innings neither gave an inch. Then,

**Above:** Mantle rounding third after he hit a sixth-inning homer that helped Yanks tie World Series at three games each. Roger Maris had homered just before Mantle's blast. St Louis' third baseman is Ken Boyer.

**Opposite:** Catcher Tim McCarver and St Louis manager Johnny Keane argue a call during the 1964 World Series. The Cards won it in seven.

in the fourth, the Cards pushed across three runs. And before the Yanks could regroup, St Louis got three more in the fifth, keyed by a Lou Brock homer. Now the Bombers had their backs against the wall, but they wouldn't quit. Mickey Mantle, showing why he was a Hall of Fame player, slammed a three-run homer in the sixth, cutting the lead in half, to 6-3. A Boyer homer off Steve Hamilton in the seventh made it 7-3, and finally the Yanks were down to their last three outs.

Showing the fatigue of pitching three games, the final two with two days rest, Gibson began to struggle. He was tagged for solo homers by Clete Boyer and Phil Linz. With two outs, Bobby Richardson was up. The little second sacker had already set a record with 13 hits in the Series. And if he got on, Roger Maris was waiting on deck, Mantle to follow.

Gibson took a deep breath, trying to coax one more out from his tired arm. He wound and threw. Richardson hit a pop fly to second base-

man Dal Maxvill, and the Cardinals were the champions, led by the young righthander whose best days were still ahead of him. Gibson had fanned 31 Yanks in 27 innings, showing that extra ounce of reserve power whenever he needed it. And despite another power performance, especially by Mantle, the Yanks had gone down to their second straight World Series defeat. Although no one knew it then, it would be the Bombers' last appearance in the fall classic for 12 long years. An era had ended for the Yankees, and a Golden Age for baseball.

The years 1941 to 1964 were particularly important ones in the history of baseball. They not only saw the game survive a world war, but they helped to usher in a new era of growth and expansion, as well as introducing a host of very great ballplayers who paved the way for the modern era of the 1970s and 1980s.

It was an age in which one team dominated the game as no team has before or since, or probably ever will. Between 1941 and 1964 the New York Yankees won the American League pennant 18 times and the World Series on 12 occasions. But after 1964 the string began running out. Mantle succumbed to one nagging injury after another, ceased to be a force and was out of baseball after 1968. By 1964 the team had slumped to sixth, at 77-85, and a year later they finished dead last in the American League, with a 70-89 mark.

But during this Golden Age of the game so many individual players left behind memories and thrills never to be forgotten. At the beginning there were DiMaggio, Musial, Williams and Feller. Then there was Jackie Robinson, perhaps bridging the biggest gap the sport had known. He was followed by the likes of Mantle, Mays, Aaron, Clemente, Frank Robinson, Banks, Ford, Koufax and Marichal. And the changing of the guard would continue. When the era ended in 1964 the likes of Rose, Yastrzemski, Gibson, McCovey, Brock and Oliva were just getting started.

The records that were left behind are still talked about. DiMaggio's 56-game hitting streak, Williams' .406 batting average, Maris' 61 homers, Spahn's 363 lifetime victories. Some, such as Wills' 104 steals, have since been broken, but are no less great in their own right.

And look at the great sluggers that came out of the era. Henry Aaron would finish his career with 755 round trippers, Mays with 660, Frank Robinson with 586, Killebrew with 573, Mantle with 536, Williams and McCovey with 521, Mathews and Banks with 512. How these men could hit a baseball!

To some who have only read about the period it may already seem like long ago, a distant past.

But to those baseball fans who actually lived through it, the memories are more than vivid. Who can forget Stan Musial and his peek-a-boo stance, Willie Mays running out from under his cap, Jackie Robinson stealing home, Mickey Mantle hitting homers that looked as if they'd never come down, Bob Feller and Sandy Koufax blazing their fastballs, Maury Wills and Lou Brock flashing across the basepaths, Ted Williams just looking as if he was born to hit.

Oh, yes, it was a Golden Age, a part of baseball to be forever cherished and remembered. It was a special time, with special players, and it helped forge the future of the game in hundreds of big and little ways. It was the culmination of all that had gone before and the dawn of the modern game that so excites us today. Other Golden Ages may lie in baseball's future, but they will have to be extraordinary indeed to surpass the one we have already had.

# INDEX

## ACKNOWLEDGMENTS

The author and publisher would like to thank the following people who helped in the preparation of this book: John Kirk the editor; Mike Rose, the designer; Rita Longabucco and Donna Cornell Muntz, the picture editors; and Cynthia Klein, who prepared the index.


## PICTURE CREDITS

The Bettmann Archive, Inc: 9(top).
National Baseball Library, Cooperstown, NY: 11, 13(top, bottom), 14, 15(top), 22, 23(right), 27(top), 28(bottom left, bottom right), 30(left), 32(top), 33(top, bottom), 34(bottom), 38(top left, top right, bottom right), 44(top, bottom), 41(left), 42(top), 43(top), 51(top right), 53(center, bottom), 54(bottom), 55(top left), 56(bottom), 65(top), 67(top), 68, 70(right), 71, 72, 79(top), 82(top), 83, 84(top), 86(bottom), 89(top), 90(top), 96(bottom), 100(bottom), 107, 108(bottom left, top right), 109, 110(bottom), 112(bottom), 114(bottom left, top right), 115(top), 120(right), 121(bottom), 125, 127(right), 131, 134(bottom), 135(top), 146(top right, bottom), 149(bottom), 161(top, bottom), 166 (top, bottom), 167, 169(bottom), 174(top, bottom), 179(bottom), 180, 181(top), 182(bottom).
UPI/Bettmann Newsphotos: 6(left, right), 7(top, bottom), 8(top, bottom), 9, 12, 15(bottom left, bottom right), 16, 17(top, bottom), 18(left), 18-19(bottom), 19(top, bottom right), 21, 22-23(bottom), 24(top, bottom), 25(top, bottom), 26-27, 28(top), 29, 30(right), 31(top, bottom), 32(bottom), 34(top), 35, 37, 40, 41(right), 42(bottom), 43(bottom), 44, 45, 46(top, bottom), 47, 48(top, bottom), 49, 50, 51(top left, bottom), 52, 53(top), 54(top), 55(top right, bottom), 56(top), 57, 58, 59, 61, 62, 63(top, bottom), 64(top, bottom), 64-65(bottom), 66(top, bottom), 67(bottom), 69(top, bottom), 70(left), 73(top, bottom left, bottom right), 74(top, bottom), 75(top, bottom), 76, 77(top, bottom), 78(top, bottom), 79(bottom), 81, 82(bottom), 84(bottom), 85, 86(top), 87, 88(top, bottom), 89(bottom), 90(bottom), 91(top, bottom), 92, 93(top, bottom), 94(top, bottom), 95(top, bottom), 96(top), 97(top, bottom), 98(top, bottom), 99, 100(top), 101(top, bottom), 102, 103(top, bottom), 104, 105, 110(top), 111(top, bottom), 112(top), 113, 115(bottom), 116, 117(top, bottom), 118(top, bottom), 119(top, bottom), 120(left), 121(top), 122, 123(top, bottom), 124(top, bottom), 126, 127(left), 128(top, bottom), 129(top, bottom), 130(top, bottom), 132-133, 134(top), 135(bottom), 136(top, bottom), 137, 138(top, bottom), 139(top, bottom), 140(top, bottom), 141, 142, 143, 144(bottom left, top right), 145, 146(top left), 147, 148, 149(top), 150, 151, 151(inset), 152(top, bottom), 153, 155, 156, 157(top, bottom), 158, 159(top, bottom), 160, 162(top), 162-163(bottom), 163(top), 164, 165(top, bottom), 168(top, bottom), 169(top), 170, 171(top, bottom), 172-173, 175, 176(top, bottom), 177(top, bottom), 178(top, bottom), 179(top), 181(bottom), 182(top), 183(top, bottom), 184(top, bottom), 184-185, 186, 187, 188, 189.
US Marine Corps: 27(bottom).
US Navy: 23(top left).